COACHING
training

ATD Workshop Series

COACHING
training

LISA HANEBERG

atd
PRESS

Alexandria, Virginia

ATD Press is an internationally renowned source of insightful and practical information on talent development, workplace learning, and professional development.

ATD Press
1640 King Street
Alexandria, VA 22314

Ordering information for print edition: Books published by ATD Press can be purchased by visiting ATD's website at td.org/books or by calling 800.628.2783 or 703.683.8100.

Library of Congress Control Number: 2015932209 (print edition only)

ISBN-10: 1-56286-967-1
ISBN-13: 978-1-56286-967-0
e-ISBN: 978-1-60728-434-5

ATD Press Editorial Staff:
Director: Kristine Luecker
Manager: Christian Green
Community of Practice Manager, Learning & Development: Amanda Smith

Project Development and Editorial Production: Jacqueline Edlund-Braun, Editorial Director, Trainers Publishing House (TPH), Fairfax, VA
Cover and Text Design: Ana Ilieva Foreman/Design
Composition: Kristin Goble, PerfecType, Nashville, TN, and Debra Deysher, Double D Media, Reading, PA
Cover art: Shutterstock
Printed by Data Reproductions Corporation, Auburn Hills, MI, www.datarepro.com

The ATD Workshop Series

Whether you are a professional trainer who needs to pull together a new training program next week, or someone who does a bit of training as a part of your job, you'll find the ATD Workshop Series is a timesaver.

Topics deliver key learning on today's most pressing business needs, including training for communication skills, leadership, coaching, new supervisors, customer service, new employee orientation, and more. The series is designed for busy training and HR professionals, consultants, and managers who need to deliver training quickly to optimize performance now.

Each ATD Workshop book provides all the content and trainer's tools you need to create and deliver compelling training guaranteed to

- **enhance** learner engagement
- **deepen** learner understanding
- **increase** learning application.

Each book in the series offers innovative and engaging programs designed by leading experts and grounded in design and delivery best practices and theory. It is like having an expert trainer helping you with each step in the workshop process. The straightforward, practical instructions help you prepare and deliver the workshops quickly and effectively. Flexible timing options allow you to choose from half-day, one-day, and two-day workshop formats, or to create your own, using the tips and strategies presented for customizing the workshops to fit your unique business environment. Each ATD Workshop book also comes with guidance on leveraging learning technologies to maximize workshop design and delivery efficiency and access to all the training materials you will need, including activities, handouts, tools, assessments, and presentation slides.

Contents

Foreword

In 2002, we launched the ASTD Trainer's WorkShop Series—a collection of books authored by practitioners that focused on the design and delivery of training on popular soft-skills topics. The creation of this series was a departure for us. These workshops-in-a-book were created to help internal trainers expedite their program delivery by using appropriate and exceptionally designed content that could be adapted and repurposed.

These topics, dealing with issues ranging from customer service to leadership to manager skills, continue to be important training programs offered in companies and organizations of all sizes and across the globe. Twelve years later the ASTD Trainer's WorkShop Series has helped more than 60,000 trainers and occasional trainers deliver top-notch programs that meet business needs and help drive performance.

And while many things about the delivery of soft skills training have not changed in the last decade, there have been advances in technology and its use in training. So, when we began talking about how to refresh this popular series, we knew we needed to incorporate technology and new topics. We also wanted to make sure that the new series was cohesively designed and had input from author-practitioners who are, after all, the heart and soul of this series.

I am pleased to announce the re-launch of a brand-new ATD Workshop Series. It is only appropriate that this new series is publishing under our new ATD banner. Inside *Coaching Training* by Lisa Haneberg, and each of the titles in the series, you'll find innovative content and fresh program agendas to simplify your delivery of key training topics. You'll also find consistency between titles, with each presented in a contemporary manner, designed by peers, and reflecting the preferences of training professionals who conduct workshops.

We hope that you find tremendous value in the ATD Workshop Series.

Tony Bingham
President & CEO
Association for Talent Development (ATD)
March 2015

How to Use This Book

What's in This Chapter

- Why coaching matters
- What you need to know about training
- Estimates of time required
- A broad overview of what the book includes

Why Does Coaching Matter?

We want our employees to grow and do their best work. Adult learning, however, is not a straightforward concept. We each have different learning styles and preferences, and we come to learning with years of baggage that can lead to inaccurate assumptions, hang-ups, and unhelpful beliefs. While classroom learning is an important tool to help employees grow, the majority of learning will not occur there. Coaching is an excellent method to accelerate an individual's growth and application of new skills because it offers personalized support that can cut through these common learning barriers.

Think of coaching as bespoke learning—made to order. Great coaching is just what performers need, right when they need it—that nudge outside the box or the encouragement to go for a new promotion. Coaching is special, noble, and highly satisfying because when we focus on helping performers make progress, our contribution to individuals and organizations skyrockets.

Simply put, coaching has the power to catalyze breakthroughs in individual performance—when it is done well.

Great coaching is a powerful learning tool and an important part of any learning strategy, but it will be a waste of time and resources if not done well. You have likely received ineffective coaching at some point in your career. From coaches who seemed more interested in telling their stories and pushing their advice. From coaches who have been certified in a 10-step coaching process they mechanically use without deviation. From coaches who fail to inspire bigger thinking or pull you into the conversation. These coaching sessions don't help, won't work, and will fail to be worth either the performer's or the coach's precious time.

The workshops in this book focus on teaching coaches the essential skills needed to conduct coaching conversations that help performers grow. The focus is on helping performers based on what they most need. It's a service-oriented approach that emphasizes deep listening and encourages the performer to own and pull the coaching conversation forward. The skills that your training participants will learn after attending these courses will help them to be better coaches, leaders, and partners.

What Do I Need to Know About Training?

The ATD Workshop Series is designed to be adaptable for many levels of both training facilitation and topic expertise. Circle the answers below that most closely align with your levels of expertise and your organization's commitment to learning. Each question circled in the column labeled 3 gets three points, and so on. Sum up your total score.

If you scored 1-3 (novice at both training and topic): Your best bet is to stick closely to the materials as they are designed. Spend extra time with the content to learn as much as possible

QUICK ASSESSMENT: HOW EXPERT DO I NEED TO BE?			
Question	3	2	1
What is your expertise as a facilitator?	Expert (more than 5 years, always awesome evaluations)	Some experience (1–5 years, sometimes talk too much)	Beginner (less than 1 year, no idea what to do)
How familiar are you with the topic?	Evolving expert (have taken courses, read books, created materials, *and* it is my passion)	Some experience (have taken courses, read books, created materials)	Beginner (had a course in school)
How committed is your company to investing in training or performance improvement?	Integral part of our corporate culture	Depends on the topic—this one is hot right now	Cheap and fast
TOTAL:			

about it. Also, closely read Chapter 8 on training delivery and consider practicing with a colleague before delivering the program.

If you scored 4-6 (topic expert): Use the outline and materials, but feel free to include materials you have developed and believe are relevant to the topic.

If you scored 7-9 (training expert): Feel free to adapt the agendas and materials as you see fit and use any materials that you have already developed, or simply incorporate training activities, tools, handouts, and so forth into your own agenda.

For more on facilitation skills, see Chapter 8 in this volume. Chapter 13 includes a comprehensive assessment instrument that will help you manage your professional development and increase the effectiveness of your coaching training sessions (see Assessment 3: Facilitator Competencies).

How Much Time Will Preparation Take?

Putting together and facilitating a training workshop, even when the agendas, activities, tools, and assessments are created for you, can be time consuming. For planning purposes, estimate about four days preparation time for a two-day course.

What Are the Important Features of the Book?

Section I includes the various workshop designs (from half-day to two days) with agendas and thumbnails from presentation slides as well as a chapter on customizing the workshop for your circumstances. The chapters included are

- Chapter 1. Two-Day Workshop (15 hours program time) + Agenda + PPT (thumbnails)
- Chapter 2. One-Day Workshop (7.5 hours program time) + Agenda + PPT (thumbnails)
- Chapter 3. Half-Day Workshop (3 to 4 hours program time) + Agenda + PPT (thumbnails)
- Chapter 4. Customizing the Coaching Training Workshop.

The workshop chapters include advice, instructions, workshop at-a-glance tables, as well as full program agendas.

Section II is standard from book to book in the ATD Workshop Series as a way to provide a consistent foundation of training principles. This section's chapters follow the ADDIE model—the classic instructional design model named after its steps (analysis, design, development, implementation, and evaluation). The chapters are based on best practices and crafted with input from experienced training practitioners. They are meant to help you get up to speed as quickly as possible. Each chapter includes several additional recurring features to help you understand the concepts and ideas presented. The Bare Minimum gives you the bare bones of what you need to know about the topic. Key Points summarize the most important points of each chapter. What to Do Next guides you to your next action steps. And, finally, the Additional Resources section at the end of each chapter gives you options for further reading to broaden your understanding of training design and delivery. Section II chapters include

- Chapter 5. Identifying Needs for Coaching Training
- Chapter 6. Understanding the Foundations of Training Design
- Chapter 7. Leveraging Technology to Maximize and Support Design and Delivery
- Chapter 8. Delivering Your Coaching Workshop: Be a Great Facilitator
- Chapter 9. Evaluating Workshop Results.

Section III covers information about post-workshop learning:

- Chapter 10. The Follow-Up Coach
- Chapter 11. Follow-Up Activities

Section IV includes all the supporting documents and online guidance:

- Chapter 12. Learning Activities
- Chapter 13. Assessments
- Chapter 14. Handouts
- Chapter 15. Online Tools and Downloads.

The book includes everything you need to prepare for and deliver your workshop:

- **Agendas,** the heart of the series, are laid out in three columns for ease of delivery. The first column shows the timing, the second gives the presentation slide number and image for quick reference, and the third gives instructions and facilitation notes. These are designed to be straightforward, simple agendas that you can take into the training room and use to stay on track. They include cues on the learning activities, notes about tools or handouts to include, and other important delivery tips. You can download the agendas from the website (see Chapter 15) and print them out for easy use.

- **Learning activities,** which are more detailed than the agendas, cover the objectives of the activity, the time and materials required, the steps involved, variations on the activity in some cases, and wrap-up or debriefing questions or comments.

- **Assessments, handouts, and tools** are the training materials you will provide to learners to support the training program. These can include scorecards for games, instructions, reference materials, samples, self-assessments, and so forth.
- **Presentation media** (PowerPoint slides) are deliberately designed to be simple so that you can customize them for your company and context. They are provided for your convenience. Chapter 7 discusses different forms of technology that you can incorporate into your program, including different types of presentation media.

All the program materials are available for download, customization, and duplication. See Chapter 15 for instructions on how to access the materials.

How Are the Agendas Laid Out?

The following agenda is a short sample of the two-day coaching skills workshop agenda.

Day One: (8:00 a.m. to 4:00 p.m.)

TIMING	SLIDES	ACTIVITIES/NOTES/CONSIDERATIONS
Before the workshop (60 min)		**Workshop Setup**
		Set up the room so that participants are seated in groups of 4 to 6 people.
		Ensure you have all your handouts copied and other supplies. Place sticky notes, pens, and markers in the middle of each table.
		Arrange for any food and beverages. It is nice to have a bowl of hard candy in the middle of each table. (You may want to include a sugar-free option as well.)
		Put two flipcharts in the front of the room with the following headings:
		Goals
		Burning Questions
		You will also need other flipcharts later in the workshop with these headings:
		Ways to Increase Pull in Conversations
		What Does Coaching Feel Like?

TIMING	SLIDES	ACTIVITIES/NOTES/CONSIDERATIONS
8:00 a.m. (10 min)	Slide 1 **ATD** Workshop Coaching Skills Two-Day Workshop	**Welcome and Introductions** Welcome everyone as they arrive. Briefly introduce yourself. (Slide 1 of 3)
	Slide 2 Workshop Objectives · Define what great coaching is and know what it looks like in practice. · Determine your role as a coach and the role of the performer. · Learn a model of coaching and practice several key coaching skills. · Build your self-awareness as a coach and a performer and increase your confidence and interest in coaching.	**Welcome and Introductions** Review the objectives for the workshop. Set the stage for it to be participative and immediately applicable when participants go back to their workplaces. (Slide 2 of 3)

	Slide 3
	
	Workshop Agenda
	· Day 1:
	  · Introductions
	  · What Is coaching?
	  · The Coaching Model
	  · Roles: The Coach and the Performer
	  · Coachability Skills
	· Day 2:
	  · Conversation Skills
	  · Perspective Skills
	  · Progress Skills
	  · Practice Sessions
		Welcome and Introductions
		
		Review the workshop agenda. If you have favorite ground rules that you use for other courses, feel free to share them here. Otherwise, go over basic expectations and logistics (restrooms, exits, no texting, and so on).
		
		(Slide 3 of 3)

8:10 a.m.
(35 min)
	Slide 4
	
	My Coaching Story
	1. Answer the following:
	  · Your name and role
	  · Your coaching story
	    ✓ Experience giving & receiving coaching or impression of coaching
	    ✓ Goal you would like to discuss with a coach
	    ✓ Burning question related to coaching
	2. Post "Goal" and "Burning Question" on respective flipcharts (on separate sticky notes).
		Opener/Learning Activity 1: My Coaching Story
		
		This icebreaker will help participants get to know each other and start talking about coaching. Use the instructions in the learning activity and on the slide to facilitate the exercise.
		
		Lead a 10-minute group debrief using the questions in the learning activity.
		
		Let participants know that you will refer back to the charts created in this exercise throughout the workshop.

How Do I Use This Book?

If you've ever read a "Choose Your Own Adventure" book, you will recognize that this book follows a similar principle. Think back to the self-assessment at the beginning of this introduction:

- If you chose *training expert*, you can get right to work preparing one of the workshops in Section I. Use Section II as a reference. Each of the chapters features a sidebar or other information written by the author who has much experience in the topic under consideration. This advice can help guide your preparation, delivery, and evaluation of training.

- If you chose *topic expert*, read Section II in depth and skim the topic content.

- If you chose *novice at training and the topic*, then spend some serious time familiarizing yourself with both Sections I and II.

Once you have a general sense of the material, assemble your workshop. Select the appropriate agenda and then modify the times and training activities as needed and desired. Assemble the materials and familiarize yourself with the topic, the activities, and the presentation media.

Key Points

- Coaching is an important and powerful learning method when it is service oriented and performer driven.

- Deep listening skills help build positive coaching relationships.

- The workshops in this book are designed to be effective at all levels of trainer expertise.

- Good training requires an investment of time.

- The book contains everything you need to create a workshop, including agendas, learning activities, presentation media, assessments, handouts, and tools.

What to Do Next

- Review the agendas presented in Section I and select the best fit for your requirements, time constraints, and budget.

- Based on your level of expertise, skim or read in-depth the chapters in Section II.

- Consider what kind of follow-up learning activities you will want to include with the workshop by reviewing Section III.

Additional Resources

Biech, E. (2008). *10 Steps to Successful Training.* Alexandria, VA: ASTD Press.

Biech, E., ed. (2014). *ASTD Handbook: The Definitive Reference for Training & Development,* 2nd edition. Alexandria, VA: ASTD Press.

Emerson, T., and M. Stewart. (2011). *The Learning and Development Book.* Alexandria, VA: ASTD Press.

McCain, D.V., and D.D. Tobey. (2004). *Facilitation Basics.* Alexandria, VA: ASTD Press.

Piskurich, G. (2003). *Trainer Basics.* Alexandria, VA: ASTD Press.

Stolovitch, H.D., and E.J. Keeps. (2011). *Telling Ain't Training,* 2nd edition. Alexandria, VA: ASTD Press.

SECTION I

The Workshops

Chapter 1
Two-Day Coaching Workshop

What's in This Chapter

- Background of the coaching model
- Objectives of the two-day Coaching Workshop
- Summary chart for the flow of content and activities
- Two-day program agenda

This two-day Coaching Workshop will ensure that your coaches have a good foundation in how to conduct coaching conversations that help performers improve. More than half the workshop is exercises and practice sessions because the best way to learn how to coach is to either give it or receive it. The exercises start easy and then progress to participants giving and receiving a complete coaching conversation. As is the case with any active training session longer than a couple of hours, you should consider pairing up with another facilitator to maintain workshop pace, clarity, and energy.

The Backstory for the Coaching Model

The Coaching Model used for this course addresses the top needs of performers. It is not a linear or prescriptive process because a great coaching conversation always starts where the performer is (not the step in the coaching process where you left off last time). In some ways, this model might be more difficult for your training participants because it doesn't offer a simple eight-step list of things to do to be a better coach. Let's be clear; there is no eight-step list of things a coach can do to get better. Coaching is a service-oriented conversation and so must emerge from the needs of the performer.

If your training participants seem a bit unclear as to what they should "do" when coaching, reinforce the bottom line—do whatever will best help performers make progress and do it in a way that maintains the performers' ownership of their success.

Consider the example of two well-known brands to illustrate the fundamental belief upon which this Coaching Model is based. Ritz-Carlton hotels are renowned for their world-class service. When you stay at one of their hotels, you get what you need, when you need it, from professionals who make you feel great at every step in the service process. Now let's think about going to an Apple Store and signing up for an appointment with a Genius (Apple's term for its product experts). When it is your turn at the Genius Bar, you share your issue or question and the Genius tells you what's going on and how to solve your problem. At the Ritz-Carlton, the guest is the focus. At the Genius Bar, the Genius is. Our model of coaching should make performers feel more like they are staying at the Ritz-Carlton than sitting at the Genius Bar— high on customized service and low on advice. This is not to say that we don't all need a visit to our corporate Genius Bar every now and then—we do. But that's not what great coaching is about. In the introduction, coaching was described as a bespoke conversation. That's what Ritz-Carlton is known for: made-to-order service. And that's what your coaches will be known for after practicing these skills and methods.

A Note About Pre-Work

It is always a good idea to use a short pre-work assignment to get participants thinking about the topic in a new way. This course includes a very brief pre-work assignment of two simple questions:

- Recall the best coaching you have ever received. Why was it so helpful?
- When you want to ask for coaching, who do you go to and why?

Include these questions in any confirmation or reminder messages you send to participants before the course. You will find other ideas for pre-work in Chapter 4: Customizing the Coaching Training Workshop.

A Note About the Presentation Slides, Facilitator's Notes, and Key Distinctions

The presentation slides for this workshop have been designed based on two assumptions. The first assumption is that when you begin delivering this workshop, you will want all the help you can get! With this in mind, the presentation slides contain many verbal cues to help you facilitate the course well right from the start. The second assumption is that you will want to reduce the number of words or slides as you get more familiar with the course. When designing a course for others to facilitate, I always start with a slide deck that offers a lot of help, complete with full phrases or sentences (not just bullet points) so that you can convey the idea even before the material has become second nature to you. I expect that you will, in time, modify the slides to be less wordy.

Because the slides contain many verbal cues, the facilitator notes do not contain verbatim talking points, scripts, or transitions. After more than 30 years of delivering training, I know this to be true:

> Trainers who parrot talking points are not effective.

It is much better to use your own words and even fumble a bit than to use my words and sound like a robot. In addition, when you need to form the thought yourself, you "think" more about the content and how it applies to your audience.

You will notice throughout the agenda that I refer to Key Distinctions. Key Distinctions are the fundamental beliefs for the workshop and for good coaching. Together, the Key Distinctions offer a mindset about coaching that will serve participants well.

Two-Day Workshop Objectives

By the end of the two-day workshop, participants will be able to

- Define what great coaching is and what it looks like in practice
- Determine their role as a coach and the role of the performer
- Learn a model of coaching and practice several key coaching skills
- Build their self-awareness as coaches and performers and increase their confidence and interest in coaching.

Two-Day Workshop Overview

Here is a quick snapshot of the key sections and timing for the workshop. Print this page out and have it with you at the front of the classroom. Add a third column with your start time, end time, and milestones in between for easy reference and workshop pacing.

Day-One Overview

TOPICS	TIMING
Workshop Setup	60 minutes
Welcome and Introductions	10 minutes
Opener/Learning Activity 1: My Coaching Story	35 minutes
Pre-Work Discussion	15 minutes
What Is Coaching? Parts One, Two, and Three	25 minutes
Key Distinctions 1 and 2	5 minutes
BREAK	**15 minutes**
Learning Activity 2: What Does Coaching Feel Like?	30 minutes
Learning Activity 3: Coaching Skills Diagnostic/Assessment 1	45 minutes
Coaching Model Overview	15 minutes
LUNCH	**45 minutes**
Coaching Roles: Coach and Performer	5 minutes
Coach's Role	5 minutes
Learning Activity 4: Listen Deeply	20 minutes
Discussion: Coach's Role	10 minutes
Performer's Role	15 minutes
Key Distinctions 3 and 4	5 minutes
Coachability Skills	20 minutes
Enhancing Coachability	10 minutes
Key Distinction 5	5 minutes
BREAK	**15 minutes**
Learning Activity 5: Coachability Scenarios	60 minutes
Learning Activity 6: Uncoachability Triggers/Assessment 2	15 minutes
Starting the Coaching Conversation	5 minutes
Learning Activity 7: Ways to Offer Coaching	20 minutes
Ways to Offer Coaching: Sample Openers and Wrap-Up	10 minutes
Key Distinction 6	5 minutes
Day-One Wrap-Up and Review	15 minutes
TOTAL (without setup)	**480 minutes (8 hours)**

Day-Two Overview

TOPICS	TIMING
Welcome and Reconnect	5 minutes
Revisit Objectives and Agenda	5 minutes
Learning Activity 8: Day-Two Warm-Up	20 minutes
Conversation Skills: Creating Pull	20 minutes
Learning Activity 9: Creating Pull	40 minutes
Key Distinction 7	5 minutes
BREAK	**15 minutes**
Conversation Skills: Ask Better Questions	10 minutes
Learning Activity 10: Ask Better Questions	10-15 minutes
Key Distinction 8	5 minutes
Learning Activity 11: First Practice Coaching Session	60 minutes
LUNCH	**45 minutes**
Perspective Skills	20 minutes
Learning Activity 12: Critical Thinking Exercise	40 minutes
Key Distinction 9	5 minutes
Progress Skills	30 minutes
Key Distinction 10	5 minutes
Seek Coaching	5 minutes
BREAK	**15 minutes**
Learning Activity 13: Final Practice Coaching Session	90 minutes
Key Distinction 11	5 minutes
Day-Two Wrap-Up and Review	10 minutes
Key Distinctions Roundup	10 minutes
Closing and Next Steps	5 minutes
TOTAL	**480 minutes (8 hours)**

Two-Day Workshop Agenda: Day One

The detailed agendas that follow will be your guide to leading the course. Use them in conjunction with the facilitator instructions found in the learning activities in Chapter 12.

Day One: (8:00 a.m. to 4:00 p.m.)

TIMING	SLIDES	ACTIVITIES/NOTES/CONSIDERATIONS
Before the workshop (60 min)		**Workshop Setup** Set up the room so that participants are seated in groups of 4 to 6 people. Ensure you have all your handouts copied and other supplies. Place sticky notes, pens, and markers in the middle of each table. Arrange for any food and beverages. It is nice to have a bowl of hard candy in the middle of each table. (You may want to include a sugar-free option as well.) Put two flipcharts in the front of the room with the following headings: • Goals • Burning Questions You will also need other flipcharts later in the workshop with these headings: • Ways to Increase Pull in Conversations • What Does Coaching Feel Like?
8:00 a.m. (10 min)	Slide 1 ATD Workshop Coaching Skills Two-Day Workshop	**Welcome and Introductions** Welcome everyone as they arrive. Briefly introduce yourself. (Slide 1 of 3)

TIMING	SLIDES	ACTIVITIES/NOTES/CONSIDERATIONS
	Slide 2 **Workshop Objectives** · Define what great coaching is and know what it looks like in practice. · Determine your role as a coach and the role of the performer. · Learn a model of coaching and practice several key coaching skills. · Build your self-awareness as a coach and a performer and increase your confidence and interest in coaching.	**Welcome and Introductions** Review the objectives for the workshop. Set the stage for it to be participative and immediately applicable when participants go back to their workplaces. (Slide 2 of 3)

	Slide 3
	
	Workshop Agenda
	· Day 1:
	  · Introductions
	  · What Is coaching?
	  · The Coaching Model
	  · Roles: The Coach and the Performer
	  · Coachability Skills
	· Day 2:
	  · Conversation Skills
	  · Perspective Skills
	  · Progress Skills
	  · Practice Sessions
		Welcome and Introductions
		
		Review the workshop agenda. If you have favorite ground rules that you use for other courses, feel free to share them here. Otherwise, go over basic expectations and logistics (restrooms, exits, no texting, and so on).
		
		(Slide 3 of 3)

8:10 a.m.
 	
(35 min)
	Slide 4
	
	My Coaching Story
	1. Answer the following:
	  · Your name and role
	  · Your coaching story
	    ✓ Experience giving & receiving coaching or impression of coaching
	    ✓ Goal you would like to discuss with a coach
	    ✓ Burning question related to coaching
	2. Post "Goal" and "Burning Question" on respective flipcharts (on separate sticky notes).
		Opener/Learning Activity 1: My Coaching Story
		
		This icebreaker will help participants get to know each other and start talking about coaching. Use the instructions in the learning activity and on the slide to facilitate the exercise.
		
		Lead a 10-minute group debrief using the questions in the learning activity.
		
		Let participants know that you will refer back to the charts created in this exercise throughout the workshop.

8:45 a.m. (15 min)	Slide 5 **Pre-Work Discussion** For pre-work, you were asked to consider two questions: 1. Recall the best coaching you have ever received. Why was it so helpful? 2. When you want to ask for coaching, who do you go to and why? (Don't share names here, focus on the characteristics of this individual that makes him or her your preferred source for coaching.)	**Pre-Work Discussion** Ideally, you will have sent these questions to your participants as pre-work before the workshop. But even if you haven't, you can still introduce and discuss them now. Encourage participants to share their answers with the group.

TIMING	SLIDES	ACTIVITIES/NOTES/CONSIDERATIONS
9:00 a.m. (10 min)	Slide 6 **What Is Coaching?**	**Learning Content/Lecture** **What Is Coaching? Part One** Use this slide to begin the discussion of what we mean by coaching in this workshop. Many people are confused by the term *coaching*. Feel free to adjust these terms to fit your specific work culture. (Slide 1 of 4)
	Slide 7 Coaching is not the same thing as *advice* or *counseling*. Coaching / Advice / Counseling	**Learning Content/Lecture** **What Is Coaching? Part One** Some conversations, such as advice or counseling, overlap with coaching, but it is important to understand that they are not the same. (Slide 2 of 4)
	Slide 8 How are coaching, counseling, and advice similar? Coaching / To Help / Advice / Counseling	**Learning Content/Lecture** **What Is Coaching? Part One** Discuss briefly how coaching, advice, and counseling are similar. (Slide 3 of 4)
	Slide 9 How are coaching, counseling, and advice different?	**Learning Content/Lecture** **What Is Coaching? Part One** It is equally important to recognize the differences, especially as related to control (who's driving the discussion). A key point to share as you discuss this slide is that many types of conversations are designed to help the performer, but most are not driven by the performer the way great coaching is. (Slide 4 of 4)

TIMING	SLIDES	ACTIVITIES/NOTES/CONSIDERATIONS
9:10 a.m. (10 min)	Slide 10 Coaching is not the same thing as *training* or *mentoring*.	**Learning Content/Lecture** **What Is Coaching? Part Two** Continue to refine the definition of coaching with participants. Many workplaces do not distinguish among coaching, mentoring, and training, or have a different way to define them. Feel free to adjust the discussion here to match your definitions, noting that there is a lot of overlap among the three. (Slide 1 of 3)
	Slide 11 How are coaching, training, and mentoring different?	**Learning Content/Lecture** **What Is Coaching? Part Two** Use Slide 11 to review how coaching, training, and mentoring differ. (Slide 2 of 3)
	Slide 12 Many types of conversations aim at helping the performer. Coaching is the most performer-focused.	**Learning Content/Lecture** **What Is Coaching? Part Two** Use Slide 12 to make the key point that we often *think* we are coaching when we are actually giving advice or counseling. (Slide 3 of 3)
9:20 a.m. (5 min)	Slide 13 So, coaching . . . - Is a service-oriented discussion - Focuses on the performer's goals and interests - Can be one time or ongoing - Requires coach to "shape shift" to be most helpful - Requires the performer to lead the discussion and be coachable.	**Learning Content/Lecture** **What Is Coaching? Part Three** Present the basic definition of coaching we will be using in this workshop. (Slide 1 of 2)

TIMING	SLIDES	ACTIVITIES/NOTES/CONSIDERATIONS
	Slide 14 Coaching: Why We Love It · Coaching is a fabulous because it is 100-percent service. · A coaching conversation is a high-value-added activity well worth your effort. · Coaching can also be a bit mysterious because you might not know why some approaches work and others don't (and this might change from performer to performer).	**Learning Content/Lecture** **What Is Coaching? Part Three** Share your enthusiasm for great coaching with your participants as a very unique and helpful endeavor. Assure them that anyone can learn to be a great coach. (Slide 2 of 2)
9:25 a.m. (5 min)	Slide 15 Key Distinction 1 Coaching helps performers make progress toward their goals and intentions.	**Key Distinction 1** The Key Distinctions offer a way to think about coaching that will help build the foundation of great coaching. Review the first of the Key Distinctions with the participants. (Slide 1 of 2)
	Slide 16 Key Distinction 2 Great coaches "show up" based on what will best help the performer move forward.	**Key Distinction 2** Share Key Distinction 2, which emphasizes the service-oriented nature of coaching. (Slide 2 of 2)
9:30 a.m. (15 min)	Slide 17 Break	**Break**

TIMING	SLIDES	ACTIVITIES/NOTES/CONSIDERATIONS

9:45 a.m. (30 min)	Slide 18
	
	What Does Coaching Feel Like?
	
	Working in discussion groups of 2 or 3, take 10 minutes to think about the last time you received coaching the way we have defined it and answer this question:
	
	• **What did it feel like?**
	  - If you cannot recall coaching you have received, imagine what it would feel like.
	  - Write your response to this question on a large sticky note and post on the chart.
	
	© 2015 ATD. Used with permission · SLIDE 4-8
		Learning Activity 2: What Does Coaching Feel Like?
		
		Confirm that participants now understand what coaching is and how it differs from other conversations often confused with coaching. Based on this new understanding, this activity will help them reflect on whether they have experienced great coaching and, if so, how it felt to receive it.
		
		The key point here is that great coaching feels very different from getting advice.
		
		Follow instructions in learning activity and on slide to facilitate the exercise.

10:15 a.m. (45 min)	Slide 19 **Coaching Skills Diagnostic** · Based on our new understanding about what great coaching looks and feels like, you will take a self-assessment to benchmark your skills as a coach. · Be candid; this instrument is only for your development and will not be collected. · Within your group, share your overall impression about your coaching skills as a result of taking the self-assessment. © 2015 ATD. Used with permission · SLIDE 4-9	**Learning Activity 3: Coaching Skills Diagnostic** • **Assessment 1: Coaching Skills Diagnostic** Set up exercise as an informal baseline self-assessment. No one should feel like they ought to "ace" this. Even experienced coaches have underdeveloped skills based on this workshop's tougher definition of coaching (anyone can give advice!). Debrief the activity by asking participants to first discuss their overall impression of their coaching skills with their table group. Lead a large group discussion using the questions in the learning activity.

TIMING	SLIDES	ACTIVITIES/NOTES/CONSIDERATIONS
11:00 a.m. (15 min)	Slide 20 Coaching Model	**Learning Content/Lecture** **Coaching Model Overview** • **Handout 1: Coaching Model** Introduce the Coaching Model (Handout 1). Spend some time getting their reactions to it, but don't define each box because you will do that with the participants throughout the workshop. For now, ask them what's different about this Coaching Model and others they might have seen. Share some initial thoughts on the model. Include the idea that the model seems to treat relationship actions as outcomes. You can provide a very basic understanding of some of the terms used in the model but don't describe them too fully at this point. (Slide 1 of 2)
	Slide 21 Coaching Model Our model focuses on the essence of great coaching—those behaviors and practices that set coaches who make a big impact apart from those who don't.	**Learning Content/Lecture** **Coaching Model Overview** Great coaching is not about certification or following some prescribed process. Based on our definition, a prescribed process would not work because the performer might actually need something different than the process can give. So, our model here is both more difficult (checklists are easier) and less difficult (no set practices). It focuses on great coaching—those behaviors and practices that enable great coaches to make a big impact on performers and teams. (Slide 2 of 2)
11:15 a.m. (45 min)	Slide 22 Lunch	**Lunch**

TIMING	SLIDES	ACTIVITIES/NOTES/CONSIDERATIONS
12:00 p.m. (5 min)	Slide 23 We are calling ourselves "coaches" and "performers" to emphasize the ownership role that those who receive coaching hold. Terms such as *protégé* and *coachee* emphasize the coach as expert. Coaching Roles	**Learning Content/Lecture** **Coaching Roles: Coach and Performer** • **Handout 2: Coaching Roles** Begin the review of the model with roles. Clarify that you will be calling the players *coaches* and *performers* rather than terms such as *protégé* or *coachee*. *Performer* places the emphasis in the right place—on the person receiving the coaching, not on the coach.

12:05 p.m.
 	
(5 min)
	Slide 24
	
	The Coach's Role
	· **Listen deeply; show interest.**
	· **Provide great service.**
	· Offer coaching; say "yes" to coaching.
	· Do what you can to help performers:
	  · Clarify their goals, needs, and interests
	  · Get unstuck
	  · Make a connection
	  · See the situation in a more beneficial way
	  · Uncover alternative paths forward
	  · Build self-awareness
	  · Move forward
		Learning Content/Lecture
		
		Coach's Role
		
		Review the coach's role. The bolded items are the most important. The other attributes are nice and help, but service orientation and showing interest are the bottom line of coaching. If coaches only did these things, they would be successful.

12:10 p.m.
 	
(20 min)
	Slide 25
	
	What Does It Mean to "Listen Deeply?"
	Let's give this a try:
	· Work in pairs or trios.
	· **Speakers:**
	  · Talk about a hobby that you love and why.
	· **Listeners:**
	  · Allow yourself to be totally engrossed in the speaker's story—just listen, be interested, be fascinated.
	  · Ask probing questions if the speaker stops talking. *Keep the speaker talking.*
	  · Don't interrupt the speaker. Don't start talking until the speaker has stopped. Allow a full 1-2 seconds in between the speaker's words and yours.
		Learning Activity 4: Listen Deeply
		
		This fun, interactive activity helps participants practice showing interest in others and giving others their full attention—in other words, deep listening. As a facilitator, make sure that you have given deep listening a try so you can share your personal experiences with the participants.
		
		Use this slide to help guide the exercise for the participants. The learning activity provides the full instructions for facilitation.
		
		(Slide 1 of 2)

TIMING	SLIDES	ACTIVITIES/NOTES/CONSIDERATIONS
	Slide 26 **Deep Listening Debrief** · What does it feel like to be listened to in this way? · What does it feel like to listen in this way? · Practice listening deeply every day. You will notice a big difference in how performers relate to you. They will be more engaged and take more ownership of their goals and next actions. · Deep listening can transform a conversation—really!	**Learning Activity 4: Listen Deeply** Use the processing questions on this slide to get a feel for whether the participants went deep enough in the activity. You might hear some say that deep listening feels intimate and perhaps uncomfortable in the workplace. Deep listening is intimate, so we want to be careful not to go to the point of being creepy or making people squirm. We do, however, want to show our undivided attention and interest, which is very uncommon in the workplace. Deep listening is the foundation of great coaching. (Slide 2 of 2)
12:30 p.m. (10 min)	Slide 27 **The Coach's Role** · Refer to Handout 2: Coaching Roles: For which aspect of the coach's role do you feel *least prepared*? · As performers, we often need the type of help that coaches provide. How can we be a great coach if we also need coaching?	**Discussion: Coach's Role** • **Handout 2: Coaching Roles** • **Assessment 1: Coaching Skills Diagnostic** Lead a large group discussion about how participants feel about the expectations for coaches listed in Handout 2. Use the questions on the slide as discussion starters. Then ask them to think about the requirements of the role in relation to what they learned about their own coaching skills in Assessment 1. Pay attention to the level of comfort of your participants. If they prefer small group discussion, that will work well too.
12:40 p.m. (15 min)	Slide 28 **The Performer's Role** · **Be coachable.** · **Have a goal you want to work on.** · Seek coaching. Ask for the type of help you feel you need and be open to the idea that you might need something else entirely. · Let others influence you. Use the input and ideas you receive—consider it all even if you don't use it. · Own your progress. It is not the coach's job to motivate you or hold you accountable.	**Learning Content/Lecture** **Performer's Role** The purpose of learning the performer's role is two-fold. First, coaches need to recognize when coaching will and will not be effective. Second, all coaches are also performers, and they need to be open and coachable in that role as well. Review the performer's role requirements on slide. Items in bold type are the most important. (Slide 1 of 3)

TIMING	SLIDES	ACTIVITIES/NOTES/CONSIDERATIONS
	Slide 29	**Learning Content/Discussion**
	The Performer's Role · In your previous coaching experiences, which aspect of the performer's role is modeled best (or worst)? · If a performer does not model his or her role well, should you offer coaching?	**Performer's Role** You don't want to let coaches off the hook for coaching even if the performer is not doing his or her part. Coaches should still be proactive and try. Lead a brief group discussion around questions on slide. Remind participants that if the performer does not pull into the discussion, even after the coach tries to encourage him or her to open up, then maybe the time or circumstance is not right for coaching. (Slide 2 of 3)
	Slide 30	**Learning Content/Discussion**
	The Performer's Role · **Coaching should be sought and welcomed**. Does this mean you should not "offer coaching"?	**Performer's Role** Further clarify what you meant earlier when you said that the performer owns the discussion. A key point to explore is the idea that PULL is better than PUSH. Share a few examples from your experiences (when coaches tried to push information or ideas on you and when you pulled into a coaching discussion). This pull/push distinction is also useful when discussing how to increase employee engagement. Engagement cannot be pushed. (Slide 3 of 3)
12:55 p.m. (5 min)	Slide 31	**Key Distinction 3**
	Key Distinction 3 Great coaches listen in ways that bring out the best in performers.	Share this important, yet deceptively simple, Key Distinction: Great coaches listen in ways that bring out the best in performers. (Slide 1 of 2)

TIMING	SLIDES	ACTIVITIES/NOTES/CONSIDERATIONS
	Slide 32	**Key Distinction 4**
	Key Distinction 4 · Successful performers are highly coachable; they ask for and welcome coaching. · *Bonus:* As coaches, we are also performers and need to show interest in coaching and be coachable.	This Key Distinction requires performers to pull coaching into their world. Don't forget to share the bonus. (Slide 2 of 2)
1:00 p.m. (20 min)	Slide 33	**Learning Content/Lecture** **Coachability Skills**
	The key to coaching is coachability. Coachability Skills	Now that participants have a greater understanding about the two roles in the Coaching Model, move to the four key coaching skills: coachability, conversation, perspective, and progress. This section drills down into coachability. (Slide 1 of 5)
	Slide 34	**Learning Content/Lecture** **Coachability Skills**
	Coachability · Coachability is measured by how performers interact with their environment. · It is visible and observable behavior.	Use the details on the slides in this section to ensure that participants understand the definition of the first of the essential coaching skills: coachability. (Slide 2 of 5)
	Slide 35	**Learning Content/Lecture** **Coachability Skills**
	What Coachability Looks Like · Not defensive when challenged. · Welcomes feedback and ideas for improvement. · Asks for coaching. · Considers and uses ideas offered by others. · Seeks training and development in the form of reading, classes, new assignments, and coaching from others. · Has a good sense of his or her strengths and weaknesses. · Handles failures and setbacks with grace.	*Coachability* may be a new term for some of your participants, so it can be very helpful to share what it looks like in practice. (Slide 3 of 5)

TIMING	SLIDES	ACTIVITIES/NOTES/CONSIDERATIONS
	Slide 36 **What Uncoachability Looks Like** - Does not listen to ideas offered by others - Staunchly defends current ideas and approaches - Appears to be non-receptive or not interested in coaching - Does not engage in conversations about development and interprets suggestions to develop new skills as criticism - Is dismissive of others	**Learning Content/Lecture** **Coachability Skills** Knowing what uncoachability looks like is important as well. Share what uncoachability looks like in practice. (Slide 4 of 5)
	Slide 37 **Coachability Further Defined** - People are not inherently coachable or uncoachable. Everyone has moments during which they are coachable and others during which they are not. - Coachability is a way of being that can be chosen at any given moment. - **So as a coach, what can you do to help performers be more coachable?**	**Learning Content/Lecture** **Coachability Skills** Clarify that coachability is not a permanent condition. People can change how open or closed they are to coaching in an instant. Here's an example: A speaker addressing a group of hospital leaders was being received very well until she showed she had not done her research of their industry and failed to tie her suggestion to their workplace reality. She suggested that they let everyone work any hours they chose, which was clearly not possible in a busy, structured hospital setting. In an instant, the speaker turned off a number of participants, and they became uncoachable. The final bullet will help you transition into the next section on enhancing coachability. (Slide 5 of 5)

TIMING	SLIDES	ACTIVITIES/NOTES/CONSIDERATIONS
1:20 p.m. (10 min)	Slide 38 Enhancing Coachability 1. Plan a Good Setting · **Time:** Some people are less coachable in the mornings, or at 4:30 in the afternoon. Or on Fridays. Or Mondays. · **Place:** It might be better to move outside the office to reduce interruptions. Or perhaps a private office. · **Environment:** Some people are more coachable when the conversation is ad hoc, not part of a formal meeting.	**Learning Content/Lecture** **Enhancing Coachability** Emphasize that helping performers become more coachable is a core responsibility for coaches. In fact, it might be the most important thing they do. Slides 38-41 suggest four ways to enhance coachability, complete with examples of how to implement them. Please add some of your experiences here too. Participants like real-life examples, and sharing your own stories makes you more approachable. So many things can affect whether or not a performer is coachable. As this first way to enhance coachability suggests, coaches should observe the triggers and then create an environment that both interests and engages performers. (Slide 1 of 5)
	Slide 39 Enhancing Coachability 2. Appeal to a Need · Acknowledge what the performer is trying to do. · Express confidence that the need can be met or that you have some ideas that might help. · Show empathy for the need but resist going down the "if I were in your shoes" road because doing so will likely decrease coachability.	**Learning Content/Lecture** **Enhancing Coachability** The second way to enhance coachability is to appeal to a performer's need and acknowledge what he or she is trying to do. (Slide 2 of 5)
	Slide 40 Enhancing Coachability 3. Say It So They Hear It · Match your words to how they listen. If they like to discuss things thoroughly; allow ample time. If they prefer a more direct style; be direct. · If they have acted defensively in the past, your offer should not sound like, "You need coaching." · Use the words that match their goals. If they have been talking about increasing team engagement, use that phrase as well.	**Learning Content/Lecture** **Enhancing Coachability** The third way is to match your words and delivery style to how your performer listens. (Slide 3 of 5)

TIMING	SLIDES	ACTIVITIES/NOTES/CONSIDERATIONS
	Slide 41 **Enhancing Coachability** **4. Make Things Simpler** · Coachability suffers when performers feel stuck. As part of the offer for coaching, express an interest in, and belief that, this can change. · Offer to make things simpler: "Would it help if we brainstormed ways to heighten engagement?" · Offer to relieve a burden: "My group can do the next report so your team can focus on the campaign. Would that help?"	**Learning Content/Lecture** **Enhancing Coachability** The fourth way is to help make things simpler for the performer, which is a very appealing offer for almost anyone. (Slide 4 of 5)
	Slide 42 **Who's Responsible for Coachability?** · It's the performer's job to be coachable. · *However,* if you want to be a more effective coach, you will do what you can to help the performer feel more open to your coaching!	**Learning Content/Discussion** **Enhancing Coachability** To help solidify the learning on coachability, ask the participants this question: Is it really the coach's responsibility to increase the performer's coachability? Then present and discuss Slide 42. Ask participants to share some of their own experiences with techniques to enhance coachability. Encourage them to share both positive and negative examples. (Slide 5 of 5)
1:30 p.m. (5 min)	Slide 43 **Key Distinction 5** The best coaching enabler, or lever, is coachability. If the performer is not open and ready, the coaching conversation is a waste of time. As a coach, job number one is to help enhance the performer's coachability. It's like proper hydration before and during a marathon. Without it, nothing else matters.	**Key Distinction 5** Share Key Distinction 5, which concerns the importance of coachability as a powerful coaching tool.
1:35 p.m. (15 min)	Slide 44 Break	**Break**

TIMING	SLIDES	ACTIVITIES/NOTES/CONSIDERATIONS
1:50 p.m. (60 min)	Slide 45 Coachability Scenario 1 - Bob is frustrated with the pace of progress in the team, but it seems he is not sure what to do to help the team get unstuck. - From working with Bob, you know that he can get sidetracked when he feels overwhelmed, which can make him less coachable. - How might you help "Overwhelmed Bob" be more coachable?	**Learning Activity 5: Coachability Scenarios** This activity gives participants a chance to work together in small groups to define the concept of coachability and identify ideas to improve coachability back in their workplace. Take your time with this exercise because it will help cement the ideas you have just presented. Present each scenario on the slide and then encourage groups to discuss the scenario and answer its question. Encourage groups to come up with at least three ways to improve the performer's coachability, one of which they are willing to share with the whole group. After 10-15 minutes, move to the next scenario and repeat. (Slide 1 of 3)
	Slide 46 Coachability Scenario 2 - Sally is creating a new training program, and she wants it to be great. Right now, it is OK. - You have seen Sally take simple suggestions very personally, and this reduces her openness to new ideas. - How might you help "Sensitive Sally" be more coachable?	**Learning Activity 5: Coachability Scenarios** Present Scenario 2 and encourage groups to discuss it and answer its question. After 10-15 minutes, move to the next scenario. (Slide 2 of 3)
	Slide 47 Coachability Scenario 3 - Dan has asked you for coaching on ways he can help his team be more agile and change-ready. - Others have warned you that Dan is not a morning person, but his assistant booked you for an 8:00 a.m. meeting with him. - How might you help "Not-an-Early-Bird Dan" be more coachable?	**Learning Activity 5: Coachability Scenarios** Present Scenario 3 and encourage groups to discuss it and answer its question. After 10-15 minutes, debrief the activity using the questions in the learning activity. (Slide 3 of 3)

TIMING	SLIDES	ACTIVITIES/NOTES/CONSIDERATIONS
2:50 p.m. (15 min)	Slide 48 Uncoachability Triggers - What are your coachability triggers? - Complete Assessment 2: Uncoachability Triggers Checklist. Check any trigger that has affected your coachability in the last month. - **How many did you check off?**	**Self-Assessment/Learning Activity 6: Uncoachability Triggers** • **Assessment 2: Uncoachability Triggers Checklist** It is natural that we are coachable some of the time and uncoachable others. This short exercise will help participants build self-awareness of situations that tend to affect their coachability. If they can acknowledge their triggers, they can catch and prevent themselves from becoming uncoachable.
	Slide 49 Coachability Wrap-Up - To provide the most effective coaching, take the initiative to help enhance the performer's coachability. - Coaching someone who is uncoachable is a waste of time and energy and can negatively affect the relationship.	**Learning Content/Discussion** **Coachability Wrap-Up** Debrief the activity using the questions in the learning activity as a guide. Be willing to share one of your own triggers. Remind participants that being more aware of triggers helps coaches provide the environment that improves performer coachability. Knowledge is power!
3:05 p.m. (5 min)	Slide 50 Your mission is to help. Period. Starting the Coaching Conversation	**Learning Content/Lecture** **Starting the Coaching Conversation** Use this slide to transition to the topic of how to start the coaching conversation. Many coaches might resist offering coaching because they are quite nervous about how to start the discussion. Emphasize that it is OK if they are highly imperfect in their delivery as long as they come across service oriented. It is when they come across as bossy or preachy that the offer will fall flat.
3:10 p.m. (20 min)	Slide 51 Three Ways to Offer Coaching - You will be working in groups of 2 to 3 people. - Take 10 minutes to draft three example opening lines you might use to offer coaching (Not permitted: "Can I give you some coaching?"): Be sure that lines do not sound like advice, counseling, training, or mentoring. - Although you are taking the initiative to offer coaching, make it clear in your choice of words that the performer will own the discussion and that you will play a service-oriented role. - Be ready to "perform" your opening lines in front of the class.	**Learning Activity 7: Ways to Offer Coaching** This activity enables participants to practice ways to start a coaching conversation that will engage the performer, encourage performer ownership, and enhance performer coachability. Follow the instructions for facilitation in the learning activity.

TIMING	SLIDES	ACTIVITIES/NOTES/CONSIDERATIONS
3:30 p.m. (10 min)	Slide 52 **Sample Openers** ~~"Can I give you some feedback?"~~ "I see what you are trying to achieve…" <small>© 2015 ATD. Used with permission. / SLIDE A52</small>	**Learning Content/Lecture** **Ways to Offer Coaching: Sample Openers** Slides 52-57 offer a few more examples of good and bad opening lines. Feel free to use some or all or add your own. If your participants did an amazing job with the previous exercise, you might be able to skip this section (tell them that you are doing so because they were brilliant!). Each example shows a statement crossed out. This statement tends to *push* people away (not all people, but many). The second statement is more likely to *pull* someone into the discussion (not all, but many). Each individual is different and that is why coaches need to listen deeply to tailor their approaches to the individual performer. (Slide 1 of 6)
	Slide 53 **Sample Openers** ~~"If I were in your shoes…"~~ "If it's helpful, I would be happy to do a meeting post-mortem (retrospective) with you over a latte…" <small>© 2015 ATD. Used with permission. / SLIDE A53</small>	**Learning Content/Lecture** **Ways to Offer Coaching: Sample Openers** (Slide 2 of 6)
	Slide 54 **Sample Openers** ~~"Your presentation was confusing."~~ "I was confused about the order of the next steps." <small>© 2015 ATD. Used with permission. / SLIDE A54</small>	**Learning Content/Lecture** **Ways to Offer Coaching: Sample Openers** (Slide 3 of 6)
	Slide 55 **Sample Openers** ~~"I don't want you to get defensive…"~~ "It's an amazing concept. I'd be interested in bantering about the options with you if that would be helpful." <small>© 2015 ATD. Used with permission. / SLIDE A55</small>	**Learning Content/Lecture** **Ways to Offer Coaching: Sample Openers** (Slide 4 of 6)

TIMING	SLIDES	ACTIVITIES/NOTES/CONSIDERATIONS
	Slide 56 **Sample Openers** ~~"It went fine."~~ "You are right. The meeting did not create the buy-in you were hoping for. What's your next step?"	**Learning Content/Lecture** **Ways to Offer Coaching: Sample Openers** (Slide 5 of 6)
	Slide 57 **Sample Openers** ~~"How's it going?"~~ "You seem a million miles away. Is there something I can help you with?"	**Learning Content/Lecture** **Ways to Offer Coaching: Sample Openers** (Slide 6 of 6)
	Slide 58 **Ways to Offer Coaching Wrap-Up** · Be direct and caring. · Let the performer pull the conversation forward. · Don't worry if your delivery is not perfect. Your intent will shine through.	**Learning Content/Lecture** **Ways to Offer Coaching Wrap-Up** Emphasize that the worst way to start is to never start. Encourage participants to take the initiative to provide coaching and not worry about being perfect.
3:40 p.m. (5 min)	Slide 59 Key Distinction 6 Getting into (beginning) the coaching conversation can feel awkward, but if you approach the discussion from a service orientation, you will do fine.	**Key Distinction 6** Share Key Distinction 6 to help pull together what they have been learning about ways to offer coaching.
3:45 p.m. (15 min) Ends 4:00 p.m.	Slide 60 Day-One Wrap-Up	**Day-One Wrap-Up and Review** Use Slides 60 and 61 to review briefly what you covered in today's workshop. Check in with the participants. How do they feel the workshop is going so far? (Slide 1 of 2)

TIMING	SLIDES	ACTIVITIES/NOTES/CONSIDERATIONS
	Slide 61 So far we have.... · Defined coaching, reviewed the Coaching Model, and assessed our coaching skills · Clarified the roles of the coach and performer · Learned about coachability and how to enhance the performer's openness to receive and use coaching Tomorrow we will learn about the other elements of the coaching model and practice.	**Day-One Wrap-Up and Review** Let them know what to expect tomorrow on day two of the workshop. If you have some extra time and want to help solidify the learning further, ask participants to each share one trigger that instantly makes them feel uncoachable. Then challenge them to notice their triggers in the future so that can stay open to learning. When we are uncoachable we cannot progress. (Slide 2 of 2)

What to Do Between Workshop Days

- Make notes on any questions or follow-up you need to do so you don't forget.

- Capture facilitator lessons learned from the first day of the workshop. Adjust day-two materials if needed.

- Deal with any equipment, room setup, catering, or other learning environment issues you weren't able to address during the workshop.

- Debrief with your co-facilitator, if appropriate.

- Get a good night's sleep so you can arrive early, refreshed, and ready to go for day two.

Two-Day Workshop Agenda: Day Two

Day Two: (8:00 a.m. to 4:00 p.m.)

TIMING	SLIDES	ACTIVITIES/NOTES/CONSIDERATIONS
8:00 a.m. (5 min)	Slide 62 ATD Workshop Coaching Skills Two-Day Reconnect	**Welcome and Reconnect** Arrive early to set up room and make sure everything works properly. Adjust room setup as needed. Welcome participants individually as they arrive.
8:05 a.m. (5 min)	Slide 63 Workshop Objectives - Define what great coaching is and know what it looks like in practice. - Determine your role as a coach and the role of the performer. - Learn a model of coaching and practice several key coaching skills. - Build your self-awareness as a coach and a performer and increase your confidence and interest in coaching.	**Revisit Objectives and Agenda** Briefly review objectives. There is no need to go in depth because participants will be able to do that in the warm-up activity. (Slide 1 of 2)

	Slide 64
	
	Workshop Agenda
	- Day 1:
	  Introductions
	  What Is Coaching?
	  The Coaching Model
	  Roles: The Coach and the Performer
	  Coachability Skills
	- Day 2:
	  Conversation Skills
	  Perspective Skills
	  Progress Skills
	  Practice Sessions
		Revisit Objectives and Agenda
		
		Briefly review agenda. Today they will have the opportunity to practice real coaching conversations.
		
		(Slide 2 of 2)

8:10 a.m. (20 min)	Slide 65 Warm-Up Activity - What is the most useful thing you learned during yesterday's class? - How has your perception about coaching changed?	**Learning Activity 8: Day-Two Warm-Up** This warm-up activity will help remind participants of the concepts covered yesterday without you having to do the review yourself. Follow instructions for facilitation in the learning activity.

TIMING	SLIDES	ACTIVITIES/NOTES/CONSIDERATIONS
	Slide 66 **Coaching Model** Performer's Role Conversation / Perspective Coachability / Progress Coach's Role	**Learning Content/Lecture** • **Handout 1: Coaching Model** Briefly refresh participants on the Coaching Model you are using in this workshop as a lead-in to conversation skills (Handout 1).
8:30 a.m. (20 min)	Slide 67 The Engine for Coaching Conversation Skills	**Learning Content/Lecture** **Conversation Skills: Creating Pull** Present the next quadrant of the model—conversation—the engine for coaching. (Slide 1 of 3)

	Slide 68
	
	Conversation Skills
	
	• The first and most important part of conversation skills is **deep listening**, which we have already addressed.
	• The second most important conversation skill for coaches is **inquiry**.
	  - Bottom line: Inquiry is asking questions to explore a topic.
	  - Great inquiry creates pull.
	  - To use inquiry, ask great questions.
		Learning Content/Lecture
		
		Conversation Skills: Creating Pull
		
		For the conversation portion of the model there are two key behaviors: deep listening and inquiry. Participants practiced deep listening yesterday, so this section focuses on inquiry, which has two parts: creating pull and asking great questions.
		
		(Slide 2 of 3)

	Slide 69 **Conversation Skills That Create Pull** • Provide rallying cry that "rallies" • Are evocative—encourage reflection and bring out pride • Are provocative—excite, fascinate, and intrigue • Are memorable in some way • Make people feel great—bring out their awesomeness • Improve relationships and connection • Help people see the way forward and are catalytic • Provide advocacy—pave the way with some assistance	**Learning Content/Discussion** **Conversation Skills: Creating Pull** • **Handout 3: Conversation Characteristics That Create Pull** Spend at least 15 minutes on the conversation characteristics that create pull (Slide 69 and Handout 3). Share examples of each and ask participants for theirs. Create a robust discussion and you will see their "lightbulbs" go on. This will be especially true for managers, who will see how helpful these characteristics are for team discussions. (Slide 3 of 3)

TIMING	SLIDES	ACTIVITIES/NOTES/CONSIDERATIONS
8:50 a.m. (40 min)	Slide 70 — Creating Pull Using the Handout 3: Conversation Characteristics That Create Pull, brainstorm 10 ways you could increase pull in coaching conversations. Be specific. Don't write: "Be Fascinating." Think of a few specific strategies you could use to increase fascination in a typical coaching discussion.	**Learning Activity 9: Creating Pull** • **Handout 3: Conversation Characteristics That Create Pull** This activity will help participants explore ways to increase performer engagement and ownership through techniques that use *pull* rather than *push* practices. To facilitate the exercise, follow instructions in the learning activity and refer participants to the slide. Debrief the activity with the group using discussion questions in the learning activity.
9:30 a.m. (5 min)	Slide 71 — Key Distinction 7 Pull is better than push. This is particularly true with regards to coaching, but applies to most conversations. Pull adds the right kind of energy.	**Key Distinction 7** Finish this section on creating pull in conversations by going over Key Distinction 7. This foundational learning tends to really resonate with participants: Pull is better than push.
9:35 a.m. (15 min)	Slide 72 — Break	**Break**
9:50 a.m. (10 min)	Slide 73 — Ask Better Questions Use inquiry conversations when... · Performers are stuck and are not sure how to move forward. · Performers are learning new tasks or skills. · Performers are enthusiastic about a new idea or need your help to create a plan for how to approach their work. · Performers have only partial information or could benefit from another point of view.	**Learning Activity/Lecture** **Conversation Skills: Ask Better Questions** Coaching is either listening or asking questions, so it is important to help coaches ask better questions. Inquiry conversations are appropriate when performers have a goal or interest and express some commitment and ownership. (Slide 1 of 4)

TIMING	SLIDES	ACTIVITIES/NOTES/CONSIDERATIONS
	Slide 74	**Learning Activity/Lecture**
		Conversation Skills: Ask Better Questions
		Cover the difference between closed and open-ended questions. Remind participants that great questions are open ended and help the performer think bigger and better.
		Share examples of unhelpful questions, which are generally too narrow, obvious, or patronizing:
		• Do you want your team to listen to you?
		• Are you committed to do what it takes?
		• Are you comfortable with that?
		(Slide 2 of 4)
	Slide 75	**Learning Activity/Lecture**
		Conversation Skills: Ask Better Questions
		Use this slide to share examples of better questions.
		(Slide 3 of 4)
	Slide 76	**Learning Activity/Lecture**
		Conversation Skills: Ask Better Questions
		The most common coaching conversation pitfall is getting in the way of the performer's discovery. Have some fun discussing the pitfalls of inquiry. Most people will be able to relate to these behaviors, especially as performers.
10:00 a.m. (10-15 min)	Slide 77	**Learning Activity 10: Ask Better Questions**
		Conversation Skills: Ask Better Questions
		Participants will be practicing using questions in the two coaching sessions today, so you won't need to conduct an in-depth exercise in this section. But you can give them a brief taste of crafting their own "better" questions.
		This activity will challenge coaches to brainstorm great questions in a specific coaching situation. Use the instructions in the learning activity to facilitate the exercise and lead the group debriefing discussion.

TIMING	SLIDES	ACTIVITIES/NOTES/CONSIDERATIONS
10:10 a.m. (5 min)	Slide 78 Key Distinction 8 Be provocative. Ask great questions. Coaches need to inspire and catalyze new thinking.	**Key Distinction 8** Coaches need to inspire and catalyze new thinking. They must ask great questions.
10:15 a.m. (60 min)	Slide 79 First Practice Coaching Sessions · Relax, this is going to be fun. No pressure at all. Really. · You will play both roles—performer and coach. · Start by reviewing Handout 1: Coaching Roles and then complete Handout 4: My Coaching Worksheet. (5 minutes) · Swap Handout 4 with your partner. Then prepare for your role as coach using Handout 5: Practice 1 Coaching Worksheet. (10 minutes) · Begin the coaching conversation (two rounds, with each person playing both coach and performer). (15 minutes each round; don't skimp!) · Enjoy the discussion, listen deeply (coach), and be coachable (performer).	**Learning Activity 11: First Practice Coaching Session** • **Handout 4: My Coaching Worksheet** • **Handout 5: Practice 1 Coaching Worksheet** • **Handout 2: Coaching Roles** This is the first of two practice coaching sessions to help participants experience what it is like to give and receive coaching as defined in this course. In this first session they will practice starting the coaching conversation, listening deeply, creating pull, and asking great questions. To facilitate the exercise, follow instructions in the learning activity and refer participants to Slide 79. It is important that you don't cut this practice short and that you don't let participants speed through it. If you have a large group, consider using a co-facilitator to monitor the room. Process the activity only briefly because the second coaching practice later in the workshop will continue to build their skills. Reinforce that although this coaching conversation was highly imperfect, it was helpful. This is the way it will be in real coaching situations (although they will become more comfortable over time).
11:15 a.m. (45 min)	Slide 80 Lunch	**Lunch**

TIMING	SLIDES	ACTIVITIES/NOTES/CONSIDERATIONS
12:00 p.m. (20 min)	**Slide 81** Taming the "Meaning Making" Machine Perspective Skills	**Learning Content/Lecture** **Perspective Skills** Use this slide to transition to the next quadrant of the Coaching Model, which is perspective—taming the "meaning-making" machine. (Slide 1 of 4)
	Slide 82 Perspective Skills Defined · One of the most valuable coaching services you can provide is to help performers adopt a healthy and helpful perspective about their situation. · Perspective is most needed when performers feel overwhelmed, unsuccessful, stuck, hassled, unconfident, or unworthy. · Facilitating perspective requires critical, contextual, and systems thinking.	**Learning Content/Lecture** **Perspective Skills** This can be the toughest or the easiest section of the workshop to facilitate, depending on how you approach it. Here's the easy way: Help coaches see that often the most valuable thing they can do is help performers see their situations a bit differently. That's what the model means by perspective—the way people look at and evaluate their circumstances, challenges, or opportunities. Don't worry about spending too much time explaining it. Let the exercise in the next section do the heavy lifting to help participants understand how they can help performers improve their perspectives. (Slide 2 of 4)

	Slide 83
	
	Why Performers Lack Perspective
	
	· Performers might lack perspective if they
	  · Are operating with incomplete information
	  · Have a tendency to worry about things
	  · Are living in victim mode or feeling overwhelmed, which is getting in their way of moving forward.
	· These challenges can alter the meaning performers assign to situations.
	· We are meaning-making machines!
		Learning Content/Lecture
		Perspective Skills
		
		Use Slide 83 to review the reasons why performers lack perspective.
		
		(Slide 3 of 4)

	Slide 84 How Coaches Can Help · Use critical thinking to help performers assess the situation. · Use systemic thinking to help performers see and consider connections and interdependencies. · Help performers put things in context. Nothing occurs in isolation; we work and progress in the environment.	**Learning Content/Lecture** **Perspective Skills** Use Slide 84 to review how coaches can help performers gain perspective. (Slide 4 of 4)

TIMING	SLIDES	ACTIVITIES/NOTES/CONSIDERATIONS
12:20 p.m. (40 min)	Slide 85 Critical Thinking Exercise - Let's use the Handout 6: Critical Thinking Worksheet to practice helping a performer improve his or her perspective. - At the top sheet, write a problem or challenge that you want to resolve or solve. - Switch worksheets with your partner. Take 10 minutes to interview your partner asking the questions on the worksheet (don't worry about identifying unknown data). - Switch roles and repeat the exercise.	**Learning Activity 12: Critical Thinking Exercise** • **Handout 6: Critical Thinking Worksheet** This exercise helps participants clarify what the model means by perspective and what it looks like in practice. Follow instructions in the learning activity to facilitate this exercise. (Slide 1 of 2)
	Slide 86 Critical Thinking Exercise Debrief - As the coach, what did you notice about using the worksheet questions to "interview" the performer? How did the conversation go? - As the performer, how did it feel to be asked these questions? Did you notice any coachability triggers popping up? - How do you think this type of tool can help performers improve their perspective and, as a result, enhance focus, action, and progress?	**Learning Activity 12: Critical Thinking Exercise** To test participants' understanding of the concepts of perspective and its relation to critical thinking, lead a discussion debriefing Learning Activity 12 using the discussion questions in the learning activity and on Slide 86. (Slide 2 of 2)
1:00 p.m. (5 min)	Slide 87 Key Distinction 9 Performers possess everything they need to solve their problems and make progress—but they sometimes lack perspective.	**Key Distinction 9** Present Key Distinction 9. Coaches can help performers gain perspective and clarify the best ways forward to make progress.

TIMING	SLIDES	ACTIVITIES/NOTES/CONSIDERATIONS
1:05 p.m. (30 min)	Slide 88 Intentions require progress to become accomplishments. Progress Skills	**Learning Content/Lecture** **Progress Skills** The final quadrant of the Coaching Model is progress—intentions require it to become accomplishments. For coaches, this can be a tricky part of coaching because if the performer owns the discussion, how can coaches help hold him or her accountable? This is a good question to explore because if ensuring progress is done poorly, it can turn into the reason performers disengage from the coaching. Take some time to go over the slides in this section, sharing your own examples. There is no exercise in this section because practicing the progress discussion is a big part of the final coaching session. (Slide 1 of 5)

	Slide 89
	
	Progress Skills
	• Many performers have vision but fail to produce satisfactory results because of inadequate progress.
	• Even in small amounts, progress is one of the most powerful motivators we can tap into.
	• Coaches help enable progress by
	  • Helping performers create a plan
	  • Managing agreements
	  • Inspiring action
		Learning Content/Lecture
		
		Progress Skills
		
		Define *progress* in coaching. It can be a powerful tool in the coaching toolkit. Review three ways that coaches can enable progress:
		
		• Helping performers create action plans
		
		• Managing agreements
		
		• Inspiring action.
		
		(Slide 2 of 5)

	Slide 90 Big Power in Small Actions "Of all the things that can boost emotions, motivation, and perceptions during a workday, the single most important is making progress in meaningful work. And the more frequently people experience that sense of progress, the more likely they are to be creatively productive in the long run. Whether they are trying to solve a major scientific mystery or simply produce a high-quality product or service, everyday progress—even a small win—can make all the difference in how they feel and perform."	**Learning Content/Lecture** **Progress Skills** Share quote on the power of progress from *Harvard Business Review*. Remind coaches that great results can come from small actions.

TIMING	SLIDES	ACTIVITIES/NOTES/CONSIDERATIONS
	Slide 91 **Facilitating Progress with an Action Plan** There are many ways to help performers create an action plan: - **Not ideal:** Ask them: "What are you going to do?" - **Not ideal:** Tell them: "You need to come up with an action plan." - **Better:** Help performers identify small actions that they are highly motivated to carry out and that are so simple they can easily begin to move forward.	**Learning Content/Lecture** **Progress Skills** There are many ways to help performers create action plans, but not all are ideal. Share examples on the slide of what works and what doesn't. (Slide 4 of 5)
	Slide 92 **Questions to Facilitate Progress** What's the next step? What's the first action for this step? What requests could you make to move things forward? Progress What conversations could you have, and with whom, to get things moving? What can I do to help jumpstart your progress? Think of a project you are working on that is not progressing as you would like. Which of these questions would most help you move forward? Why? Are their other questions you would ask if you were coaching "you?"	**Learning Content/Lecture** **Progress Skills** Lead a discussion of how to use great questions to help performers move forward on their action plans. (Slide 5 of 5)
1:35 p.m. (5 min)	Slide 93 **Key Distinction 10** Progress is a powerful motivator. Coaching helps facilitate progress, and even the tiniest of steps forward fuels success.	**Key Distinction 10** Share Key Distinction 10 with participants to help solidify the idea of progress as a potent motivator in the coaching process.

1:40 p.m.
 	
(5 min)
	Slide 94
	
	Great Coaches Seek Coaching
	- Be willing to go first. Practice your opening lines:
	  - "Will you help me make this better?"
	  - "I'd love to get your thoughts on my approach to this and brainstorm potential paths forward."
	  - "Play devil's advocate with me—what would the critics of this approach say and how could I win them over?"
	  - "Thank you. I am always eager to hear how others might approach things."
	  - "Can we take 10 minutes to dry run this?"
	  - "I am feeling stuck and I am wondering if this is because I am not seeing something. Would you be open to exploring that with me?"
	- Be genuinely thankful. You will get great coaching and create a culture of coachability—a win-win.
		Learning Content/Content
		
		Seek Coaching
		
		Use this slide to transition participants from the model to practice. Let participants know that you have completed the review of the Coaching Model's four essential coaching skills: coachability, conversation, perspective, and progress. Now, to improve their skills in each of the four quadrants, they need to practice giving and receiving coaching.
		
		Put simply, great coaches seek coaching. Share these two techniques for seeking coaching: 1) be willing to go first, and 2) be genuinely thankful. Review sample opening lines they can use to request coaching.

Chapter 1: **Two-Day Coaching Workshop**   43

TIMING	SLIDES	ACTIVITIES/NOTES/CONSIDERATIONS
1:45 p.m. (15 min)	Slide 95 Break	**Break**
2:00 p.m. (90 min)	Slide 96 Final Practice Coaching Sessions - You know this will be fun! - You and your new partner will play both roles—performer and coach. - Take 5 minutes to review Handout 2: Coaching Roles and then complete Handout 4: My Coaching Worksheet. - Swap Handout 4 with your partner and then prepare for your role as coach using Handout 7: Practice 2 Coaching Worksheet. (15 minutes) - Begin the coaching conversation (two rounds, with each person playing both coach and performer) (20 minutes each round; don't skimp!) - Enjoy the discussion, listen deeply (coach), and be coachable (performer).	**Learning Activity 13: Final Practice Coaching Session** • **Handout 4: My Coaching Worksheet** • **Handout 7: Practice 2 Coaching Worksheet** • **Handout 2: Coaching Roles** This is the final practice session and should bring together everything the participants have learned in the workshop so far. It requires them, as coaches, to listen deeply, create pull, ask great questions, improve coachability, provide perspective, and ensure performer progress—the complete Coaching Model. To facilitate this exercise, follow the instructions in the learning activity and refer participants to Slide 96. Participants may want to use the same coaching topic from Practice 1 (Handout 4). They will be paired up with a different person, so the coaching sessions will be different. Have extra blank copies of Handout 4 in case some participants want to select a second coaching topic. The exercise works equally well either way, and because the coaching is real, we want them to use the topic that most interests them. When you are processing this activity, ask participants how they feel about coaching now compared with before the workshop. Use debriefing questions from the learning activity to help lead the conversation.

TIMING	SLIDES	ACTIVITIES/NOTES/CONSIDERATIONS
3:30 p.m. (5 min)	Slide 97 Key Distinction 11 Coaching is a wonderful gift. If you believe in it—and seek it—you will be better at providing it. If you don't seek coaching, what message do you send to other performers?	**Key Distinction 11** Share the final Key Distinction—coaching is a gift. If you seek it, you will be better at providing it.
3:35 p.m. (10 min)	Slide 98 Day-Two Wrap-Up	**Day-Two Wrap-Up and Review** Because participants just completed the long practice session, the closing does not include action planning. Remind the participants of the journey they have gone through together to explore coaching. Start with the Coaching Model and its roles and coaching skills. (Slide 1 of 5)
	Slide 99 Workshop Objectives: How Did We Do? · Define what great coaching is and know what it looks like in practice. · Determine your role as a coach and the role of performer. · Learn a model of coaching and practice several key coaching skills. · Build your self-awareness as a coach and performer and increase your confidence and interest in coaching.	**Day-Two Wrap-Up and Review** Review the objectives and ask participants how they think they did. (Slide 2 of 5)
	Slide 100 Coaching . . . · Is a service-oriented discussion · Focuses on the performer's goals and interests · Can be one time or ongoing · Requires coach to "shape shift" to be most helpful · Requires the performer to lead the discussion and be coachable.	**Day-Two Wrap-Up and Review** Revisit the definition of coaching developed during the course of the workshop. Encourage them to explore how their ideas about coaching have changed throughout your two days together. (Slide 3 of 5)

TIMING	SLIDES	ACTIVITIES/NOTES/CONSIDERATIONS
	Slide 101 **Coaching: Why We Love It** · Coaching is a fabulous because it is 100-percent service. · A coaching conversation is a high-value-added activity well worth your effort. · Coaching can also be a bit mysterious because you might not know why some approaches work and others don't (and this might change from performer to performer).	**Day-Two Wrap-Up and Review** Stoke their enthusiasm for great coaching as a very unique and helpful endeavor. (Slide 4 of 5)
	Slide 102 **Being a coach is …** · A privilege · A joy—it feels great to help others grow · A burden—it's not easy coaching in the ways we have discussed during this workshop · The best way to maximize your impact on others	**Day-Two Wrap-Up and Review** Assure them that anyone can learn to be a coach and that this workshop is a substantial start on their journey toward being great coaches. (Slide 5 of 5)
3:45 p.m. (10 min)	Slide 103 **Key Distinctions Roundup**	**Key Distinctions Roundup** This slide brings together all 11 Key Distinctions. Read them as a way of reviewing the most important beliefs about coaching. Ask participants which distinction will be most useful for them. Share the distinction that has most affected your own perspective about coaching and why.
3:55 p.m. (5 min) End 4:00 p.m.	Slide 104 **Next Steps** · Ask for coaching often. · Start offering more coaching. · Notice your coachability triggers and what causes others to be less open. · Explore the coaching skills that you feel are least developed and vigorously use your strengths to help others.	**Closing and Next Steps** • **Handout 10: Workshop Evaluation Form** Close the workshop with a couple of suggestions about how to get more practice as a coach and a performer. Share any final details and follow-up plans (highly recommended). See Chapters 10 and 11 for ideas to follow up the training with support and activities. Be open to answering any final questions on coaching or the concepts presented in the workshop. Conduct workshop evaluations. Remind participants that their insights help facilitators get better. Use Handout 10 or your own preferred form. (Slide 1 of 2)

TIMING	SLIDES	ACTIVITIES/NOTES/CONSIDERATIONS
	Slide 105	**Closing and Next Steps**
	Thank you for your participation. Best of success!	And, finally, encourage participants to take a few moments to thank their peer coaches. That was real coaching—they should use it. Thank them for their participation and wish them best of success in their coaching! (Slide 2 of 2)

Key Points

- The overall objective of this two-day course is to provide participants with a good foundation of coaching skills.

- The learning activities and practice sessions are designed to help participants feel more confident and comfortable initiating and navigating service-oriented coaching discussions.

- The course also explores how to help coaches be more receptive to coaching so that they can be more effective in the performer role.

What to Do Next

- Determine the schedule for training classes; reserve location and any catering you may wish to provide.

- Identify and invite participants.

- Inform participants about pre-work if you will be using it in the class.

- Review the workshop objectives, activities, and handouts to plan the content you will use.

- Prepare copies of the participant materials and any activity-related "extras." Refer to Chapter 15 for information on how to access and use the supplemental materials provided for this workshop.

- Gather any "fidgets" (quiet toys such as chenille stems, koosh balls, and so on) to place on the tables for your participants. See Chapter 8 for other ideas to enhance the learning environment of your workshop.

- Prepare yourself both emotionally and physically. Make sure you have taken care of any scheduling conflicts or personal challenges (as best you can), so that you can be fully present to facilitate the class.

- If you will be co-facilitating with a partner, meet to agree on how you will split up the training parts and how you will support each other during exercises and transition points.

- Get a good night's sleep before you facilitate your workshop so that you have the energy and focus to deliver a great class!

Chapter 2
One-Day Coaching Workshop

What's in This Chapter

- Objectives of the one-day Coaching Workshop
- Background of the coaching model
- Summary chart for the flow of content and activities
- One-day program agenda

This one-day Coaching Workshop will introduce participants to coaching and give them practice providing coaching that helps performers improve. More than half the workshop is exercises and practice sessions because the best way to learn how to coach is to either give it or receive it. The exercises start easy and end with participants giving and receiving a complete coaching conversation.

The primary difference between the one-day class and the two-day class is the depth and time devoted to practicing. Although participants learn about all parts of the Coaching Model in both workshops, some activities have been omitted in the one-day workshop. If you have the time, I recommend the two-day workshop over the one-day. If that is not possible, this workshop will provide a nice foundation.

The Backstory for the Coaching Model

The Coaching Model used for this course addresses the top needs of performers. It is not a linear or prescriptive process because a great coaching conversation always starts where the performer is (not the step in the coaching process where you left off last time). In some ways, this model might be more difficult for your training participants because it doesn't offer a simple eight-step list of things to do to be a better coach. Let's be clear; there is no eight-step list of things a coach can do to get better. Coaching is a service-oriented conversation and so must emerge from the needs of the performer.

If your training participants seem a bit unclear as to what they should "do" when coaching, reinforce the bottom line—do whatever will best help performers make progress and do it in a way that maintains the performers' ownership of their success.

Consider the example of two well-known brands to illustrate the fundamental belief upon which this Coaching Model is based. Ritz-Carlton hotels are renowned for their world-class service. When you stay at one of their hotels, you get what you need, when you need it, from professionals who make you feel great at every step in the service process. Now let's think about going to an Apple Store and signing up for an appointment with a Genius (Apple's term for its product experts). When it is your turn at the Genius Bar, you share your issue or question and the Genius tells you what's going on and how to solve your problem. At the Ritz-Carlton, the guest is the focus. At the Genius Bar, the Genius is. Our model of coaching should make performers feel more like they are staying at the Ritz-Carlton than sitting at the Genius Bar—high on customized service and low on advice. This is not to say that we don't all need a visit to our corporate Genius Bar every now and then—we do. But that's not what great coaching is about. In the introduction, coaching was described as a bespoke conversation. That's what Ritz-Carlton is known for: made-to-order service. And that's what your coaches will be known for after practicing these skills and methods.

A Note About Pre-Work

It is always a good idea to use a short pre-work assignment to get participants thinking about the topic in a new way. This course includes a very brief pre-work assignment of two simple questions:

- Recall the best coaching you have ever received. Why was it so helpful?
- When you want to ask for coaching, who do you go to and why?

Include these questions in any confirmation or reminder messages you send to participants before the course. You will find other ideas for pre-work in Chapter 4: Customizing the Coaching Training Workshop.

A Note About the Presentation Slides, Facilitator's Notes, and Key Distinctions

The presentation slides for this workshop have been designed based on two assumptions. The first assumption is that when you begin delivering this workshop, you will want all the help you can get! With this in mind, the presentation slides contain many verbal cues to help you facilitate the course well right from the start. The second assumption is that you will want to reduce the number of words or slides as you get more familiar with the course. When designing a course for others to facilitate, I always start with a slide deck that offers a lot of help, complete with full phrases or sentences (not just bullet points) so that you can convey the idea even before the material has become second nature to you. I expect that you will, in time, modify the slides to be less wordy.

Because the slides contain many verbal cues, the facilitator notes do not contain verbatim talking points, scripts, or transitions. After more than 30 years of delivering training, I know this to be true:

> Trainers who parrot talking points are not effective.

It is much better to use your own words and even fumble a bit than to use my words and sound like a robot. In addition, when you need to form the thought yourself, you "think" more about the content and how it applies to your audience.

You will notice throughout the agenda that I refer to Key Distinctions. Key Distinctions are the fundamental beliefs for the workshop and for good coaching. Together, the Key Distinctions offer a mindset about coaching that will serve participants well.

One-Day Workshop Objectives

By the end of the one-day workshop, participants will be able to

- Define what great coaching is and what it looks like in practice
- Determine their role as a coach and the role of the performer

- Learn a model of coaching and practice several key coaching skills
- Build their self-awareness as coaches and performers and increase their confidence and interest in coaching.

One-Day Workshop Overview

Here is a quick snapshot of the key sections and timing for the workshop. Print this page out and have it with you at the front of the classroom. Add a third column with your start time, end times, and the milestones in between for easy reference and workshop pacing.

TOPICS	TIMING
Workshop Setup	60 minutes
Welcome and Introductions	10 minutes
Opener/Learning Activity 1: My Coaching Story	35 minutes
Pre-Work Discussion	5 minutes
What Is Coaching?	5 minutes
Key Distinctions 1 and 2	5 minutes
Learning Activity 3: Coaching Skills Diagnostic/Assessment 1	45 minutes
Coaching Model Overview	10 minutes
BREAK	**10 minutes**
Coaching Roles	5 minutes
Learning Activity 4: Listen Deeply	20 minutes
Discussion: Coach's Role	10 minutes
Performer's Role	5 minutes
Key Distinctions 3 and 4	5 minutes
Coachability Skills	5-10 minutes
Enhancing Coachability	10 minutes
Learning Activity 5: Coachability Scenarios	10 minutes
Learning Activity 6: Uncoachability Triggers	15 minutes
Key Distinction 5	5 minutes
LUNCH	**45 minutes**
Conversation Skills: Creating Pull	15 minutes
Learning Activity 9: Creating Pull	10-15 minutes
Key Distinction 6	5 minutes
Conversation Skills: Ask Better Questions	15 minutes
Learning Activity 10: Ask Better Questions	10-15 minutes
Key Distinction 7	5 minutes
Learning Activity 14: Getting Started and Asking Great Questions	30 minutes
Perspective Skills	10 minutes

Learning Activity 15: Quick Start to Critical Thinking	15-20 minutes
Key Distinction 8	5 minutes
BREAK	**10 minutes**
Progress Skills	10-15 minutes
Key Distinction 9	2 minutes
Seek Coaching	3 minutes
Learning Activity 13: Final Practice Coaching Session	55-60 minutes
Key Distinction 10	5 minutes
Wrap-Up and Review	5 minutes
Key Distinctions Roundup	5 minutes
Closing and Next Steps	5 minutes
TOTAL (without setup)	**480 minutes (8 hours)**

One-Day Workshop Agenda

The following detailed agenda will be your guide to leading the one-day course. Use it in conjunction with the facilitator instructions for the learning activities found in Chapter 12.

Day One: (8:00 a.m. to 4:00 p.m.)

TIMING	SLIDES	ACTIVITIES/NOTES/CONSIDERATIONS
Before the Workshop (60 min)		**Workshop Setup** Set up the room so that participants are seated in groups of 4 to 6 people. Ensure you have all your handouts copied and other supplies. Place sticky notes, pens, and markers in the middle of each table. Arrange for any food and beverages. It is nice to have a bowl of hard candy in the middle of each table. (You may want to include a sugar-free option as well.) Put two flipcharts in the front of the room with the following headings: • Goals • Burning Questions

TIMING	SLIDES	ACTIVITIES/NOTES/CONSIDERATIONS
8:00 a.m. (10 min)	Slide 1 ATD Workshop Coaching Skills One-Day Workshop	**Welcome and Introductions** Welcome everyone as they arrive. Briefly introduce yourself. (Slide 1 of 3)
	Slide 2 Workshop Objectives · Define what great coaching is and know what it looks like in practice. · Determine your role as a coach and the role of the performer. · Learn a model of coaching and practice several key coaching skills. · Build your self-awareness as a coach and a performer and increase your confidence and interest in coaching.	**Welcome and Introductions** Review the objectives for the workshop. Set the stage for it to be participative and immediately applicable when participants go back to their workplaces. (Slide 2 of 3)
	Slide 3 Workshop Agenda · Introductions · What Is coaching? · The Coaching Model · Roles: The coach and the performer · Coachability Skills · Conversation Skills · Perspective Skills · Progress Skills · Practice Sessions	**Welcome and Introductions** Review the workshop agenda. If you have favorite ground rules that you use for other courses, feel free to share them here. Otherwise, go over basic expectations and logistics (restrooms, exits, no texting, and so on). (Slide 3 of 3)
8:10 a.m. (35 min)	Slide 4 My Coaching Story 1. Answer the following: · Your name and role · Your coaching story ✓ Experience giving & receiving coaching or impression of coaching ✓ Goal you would like to discuss with a coach ✓ Burning question related to coaching 2. Post "Goal" and "Burning Question" on respective flipcharts (on separate sticky notes).	**Opener/Learning Activity 1: My Coaching Story** This icebreaker will help participants get to know each other and start talking about coaching. Use the instructions in the learning activity and on the slide to facilitate the exercise. Lead a 10-minute group debrief using the questions in the learning activity. Let participants know that you will refer back to the charts created in this exercise throughout the workshop.

TIMING	SLIDES	ACTIVITIES/NOTES/CONSIDERATIONS
8:45 a.m. (5 min)	Slide 5 **Pre-Work Discussion** For pre-work, you were asked to consider two questions: · Recall the best coaching you have ever received. Why was it so helpful? · When you want to ask for coaching, who do you go to and why? (Don't share names here, focus on the characteristics of this individual that makes him or her your preferred source for coaching.)	**Pre-Work Discussion** Ideally, you will have sent these questions to your participants as pre-work before the workshop. But even if you haven't, you can still introduce and discuss them now. Encourage participants to share their answers with the group.
8:50 a.m. (5 min)	Slide 6 Coaching… · Is a service-oriented discussion · Focuses on the performer's goals and interests · Can be one time or ongoing · Requires coach to "shape shift" to be most helpful · Requires the performer to lead the discussion and be coachable.	**Learning Content/Lecture** **What Is Coaching?** Many people are confused by the term *coaching*. Use this slide to present the basic definition of coaching we will be using in this workshop. If it resonates with you, share the Ritz-Carlton versus Apple story in the introduction of this chapter. Your goal for this quick introduction is to shift their mindset so that when they think about coaching, they think "flexible performer-driven service." (Slide 1 of 2)
	Slide 7 Coaching: Why We Love It · Coaching is a fabulous because it is 100-percent service. · A coaching conversation is a high-value-added activity well worth your effort. · Coaching can also be a bit mysterious because you might not know why some approaches work and others don't (and this might change from performer to performer).	**Learning Content/Lecture** **What Is Coaching?** Share your enthusiasm for great coaching with your participants as a very unique and helpful endeavor. Assure them that anyone can learn to be a great coach. (Slide 2 of 2)
8:55 a.m. (5 min)	Slide 8 Key Distinction 1 Coaching helps performers make progress toward their goals and intentions.	**Key Distinction 1** The Key Distinctions offer a way to think about coaching that will help build the foundation of great coaching. Share that you will be introducing Key Distinctions throughout the course. Review the first of the Key Distinctions with the participants. (Slide 1 of 2)

TIMING	SLIDES	ACTIVITIES/NOTES/CONSIDERATIONS
	Slide 9 **Key Distinction 2** Great coaches "show up" based on what will best help the performer move forward.	**Key Distinction 2** Share Key Distinction 2, which emphasizes the service-oriented nature of coaching. (Slide 2 of 2)
9:00 a.m. (45 min)	Slide 10 Coaching Skills Diagnostic · Based on our new understanding about what great coaching looks and feels like, you will take a self-assessment to benchmark your skills as a coach. · Be candid; this instrument is only for your development and will not be collected. · Within your group, share your overall impression about your coaching skills as a result of taking the self-assessment.	**Learning Activity 3: Coaching Skills Diagnostic** • **Assessment 1: Coaching Skills Diagnostic** Set up exercise as an informal baseline self-assessment. No one should feel like they ought to "ace" this. Even experienced coaches have underdeveloped skills based on this workshop's tougher definition of coaching (anyone can give advice!). Debrief the activity by asking participants to first discuss their overall impression of their coaching skills with their table group. Lead a large group discussion using the questions in the learning activity.
9:45 a.m. (10 min)	Slide 11 Coaching Model Performer's Role Conversation / Perspective Coachability / Progress Coach's Role	**Learning Content/Lecture** **Coaching Model Overview** • **Handout 1: Coaching Model** Introduce the Coaching Model (Handout 1). Spend some time getting their reactions to it, but don't define each box because you will do that with the participants throughout the workshop. For now, ask them what's different about this Coaching Model and others they might have seen. Share some initial thoughts on the model. Include the idea that the model seems to treat relationship actions as outcomes. You can provide a very basic understanding of some of the terms used in the model but don't describe them too fully at this point. (Slide 1 of 2)

TIMING	SLIDES	ACTIVITIES/NOTES/CONSIDERATIONS
	Slide 12	**Learning Content/Lecture**
	Coaching Model Our model focuses on the essence of great coaching—those behaviors and practices that set coaches who make a big impact apart from those who don't.	**Coaching Model Overview**
		Great coaching is not about certification or following some prescribed process. Based on our definition, a prescribed process would not work because the performer might actually need something different than the process can give. So, the model here is both more difficult (checklists are easier) and less difficult (no set practices). It focuses on great coaching—those behaviors and practices that enable great coaches to make a big impact on performers and teams.
		(Slide 2 of 2)
9:55 a.m. (10 min)	Slide 13 Break	**Break**
10:05 a.m. (5 min)	Slide 14 We are calling ourselves 'coaches' and 'performers' to emphasize the ownership role that those who receive coaching hold. Terms such as protégé and coachee emphasize the coach as expert. Coaching Roles	**Learning Content/Lecture** **Coaching Roles** • **Handout 2: Coaching Roles** Begin the review of the model with roles. Clarify that you will be calling the players *coaches* and *performers* rather than terms such as *protégé* or *coachee*. *Performer* places the emphasis in the right place—on the person receiving the coaching, not on the coach.
	Slide 15 **The Coach's Role** - **Listen deeply; show interest.** - **Provide great service.** - Offer coaching; say "yes" to coaching. - Do what you can to help performers: Clarify their goals, needs, and interests Get unstuck Make a connection See the situation in a more beneficial way Uncover alternative paths forward Build self-awareness Move forward	**Learning Content/Lecture** **Coach's Role** Review the coach's role. The bolded items are the most important. The other attributes are nice and help, but service orientation and showing interest are the bottom line of coaching. If coaches only did these things, they would be successful.

TIMING	SLIDES	ACTIVITIES/NOTES/CONSIDERATIONS
10:10 a.m. (20 min)	Slide 16 What Does It Mean to "Listen Deeply?" Let's give this a try: Work in pairs or trios. **Speakers:** Talk about a hobby that you love and why. **Listeners:** Allow yourself to be totally engrossed in the speaker's story—just listen, be interested, be fascinated. Ask probing questions if the speaker stops talking. *Keep the speaker talking.* Don't interrupt the speaker. Don't start talking until the speaker has stopped. Allow a full 1-2 seconds in between the speaker's words and yours.	**Learning Activity 4: Listen Deeply** This fun, interactive activity helps participants practice showing interest in others and giving others their full attention—in other words, deep listening. As a facilitator, make sure that you have given deep listening a try so you can share your personal experiences with the participants. Use this slide to help guide the exercise for the participants. The learning activity provides the full instructions for facilitation. (Slide 1 of 2)
	Slide 17 Deep Listening Debrief • What does it feel like to be listened to in this way? • What does it feel like to listen in this way? • Practice listening deeply every day. You will notice a big difference in how performers relate to you. They will be more engaged and take more ownership of their goals and next actions. • Deep listening can transform a conversation—really!	**Learning Activity 4: Listen Deeply** Use the processing questions on this slide to get a feel for whether the participants went deep enough in the activity. You might hear some say that deep listening feels intimate and perhaps uncomfortable in the workplace. Deep listening is intimate, so we want to be careful not to go to the point of being creepy or making people squirm. We do, however, want to show our undivided attention and interest, which is very uncommon in the workplace. Deep listening is the foundation of great coaching. (Slide 2 of 2)
10:30 a.m. (10 min)	Slide 18 The Coach's Role • Refer to Handout 2: Coaching Roles: For which aspect of the coach's role do you feel *least prepared*? • As performers, we often need the type of help that coaches provide. How can we be a great coach if we also need coaching?	**Discussion: Coach's Role** • **Handout 2: Coaching Roles** • **Assessment 1: Coaching Skills Diagnostic** Lead a large group discussion about how participants feel about the expectations for coaches listed in Handout 2. Use the questions on the slide as discussion starters. Then ask them to think about the requirements of the role in relation to what they learned about their own coaching skills in Assessment 1. Pay attention to the level of comfort of your participants. If they prefer small group discussion, that will work well too.

TIMING	SLIDES	ACTIVITIES/NOTES/CONSIDERATIONS
10:40 a.m. (5 min)	Slide 19 **The Performer's Role** · Be coachable. · Have a goal you want to work on. · Seek coaching. Ask for the type of help you feel you need and be open to the idea that you might need something else entirely. · Let others influence you. Use the input and ideas you receive—consider it all even if you don't use it. · Own your progress. It is not the coach's job to motivate you or hold you accountable.	**Learning Content/Lecture** **Performer's Role** The purpose of learning the performer's role is two-fold. First, coaches need to recognize when coaching will and will not be effective. Second, all coaches are also performers, and they need to be open and coachable in that role as well. Review the performer's role requirements on slide. Items in bold type are the most important.
10:45 a.m. (5 min)	Slide 20 **Key Distinction 3** Great coaches listen in ways that bring out the best in performers.	**Key Distinction 3** Share this important, yet deceptively simple, Key Distinction: Great coaches listen in ways that bring out the best in performers. (Slide 1 of 2)
	Slide 21 **Key Distinction 4** · Successful performers are highly coachable; they ask for and welcome coaching. · *Bonus*: As coaches, we are also performers and need to show interest in coaching and be coachable.	**Key Distinction 4** This Key Distinction requires performers to pull coaching into their world. Don't forget to share the bonus. (Slide 2 of 2)
10:50 a.m. (5-10 min)	Slide 22 The key to coaching is coachability. **Coachability Skills**	**Learning Content/Lecture** **Coachability Skills** Now that participants have a greater understanding about the two roles in the Coaching Model, move to the four key coaching skills: coachability, conversation, perspective, and progress. This next section drills down on coachability. (Slide 1 of 4)

TIMING	SLIDES	ACTIVITIES/NOTES/CONSIDERATIONS
	Slide 23 **Coachability** · Coachability is measured by how performers interact with their environment. · It is visible and observable behavior.	**Learning Content/Lecture** **Coachability Skills** Use the details on the slides in this section to ensure that participants understand the definition of the first of the essential coaching skills: coachability. (Slide 2 of 4)
	Slide 24 **What Coachability Looks Like** · Not defensive when challenged. · Welcomes feedback and ideas for improvement. · Asks for coaching. · Considers and uses ideas offered by others. · Seeks training and development in the form of reading, classes, new assignments, and coaching from others. · Has a good sense of his or her strengths and weaknesses. · Handles failures and setbacks with grace.	**Learning Content/Lecture** **Coachability Skills** *Coachability* may be a new term for some of your participants, so it can be very helpful to share what it looks like in practice. (Slide 3 of 4)
	Slide 25 **What Uncoachability Looks Like** · Does not listen to ideas offered by others · Staunchly defends current ideas and approaches · Appears to be non-receptive or not interested in coaching · Does not engage in conversations about development and interprets suggestions to develop new skills as criticism · Is dismissive of others	**Learning Content/Lecture** **Coachability Skills** Knowing what uncoachability looks like is important as well. Share what uncoachability looks like in practice. (Slide 4 of 4)

TIMING	SLIDES	ACTIVITIES/NOTES/CONSIDERATIONS
10:55 a.m. (10 min)	Slide 26 **Enhancing Coachability** **1. Plan a Good Setting** • **Time:** Some people are less coachable in the mornings, or at 4:30 in the afternoon. Or on Fridays. Or Mondays. • **Place:** It might be better to move outside the office to reduce interruptions. Or perhaps a private office. • **Environment:** Some people are more coachable when the conversation is ad hoc, not part of a formal meeting.	**Learning Content/Lecture** **Enhancing Coachability** Emphasize that helping performers become more coachable is a core responsibility for coaches. In fact, it might be the most important thing they do. Slides 26-29 suggest four ways to enhance coachability, complete with examples of how to implement them. Please add some of your experiences here too. Participants like real-life examples, and sharing your own stories makes you more approachable. So many things can affect whether or not a performer is coachable. As this first way to enhance coachability suggests, coaches should observe the triggers and then create an environment that both interests and engages performers. (Slide 1 of 5)
	Slide 27 **Enhancing Coachability** **2. Appeal to a Need** • Acknowledge what the performer is trying to do. • Express confidence that the need can be met or that you have some ideas that might help. • Show empathy for the need but resist going down the "if I were in your shoes" road because doing so will likely decrease coachability.	**Learning Content/Lecture** **Enhancing Coachability** The second way to enhance coachability is to appeal to a performer's need and acknowledge what he or she is trying to do. (Slide 2 of 5)
	Slide 28 **Enhancing Coachability** **3. Say It So They Hear It** • Match your words to how they listen. If they like to discuss things thoroughly; allow ample time. If they prefer a more direct style; be direct. • If they have acted defensively in the past, your offer should not sound like, "You need coaching." • Use the words that match their goals. If they have been talking about increasing team engagement, use that phrase as well.	**Learning Content/Lecture** **Enhancing Coachability** The third way is to match your words and delivery style to how your performer listens. (Slide 3 of 5)

TIMING	SLIDES	ACTIVITIES/NOTES/CONSIDERATIONS
	Slide 29 **Enhancing Coachability** **4. Make Things Simpler** - Coachability suffers when performers feel stuck. As part of the offer for coaching, express an interest in, and belief that, this can change. - Offer to make things simpler: "Would it help if we brainstormed ways to heighten engagement?" - Offer to relieve a burden: "My group can do the next report so your team can focus on the campaign. Would that help?"	**Learning Content/Lecture** **Enhancing Coachability** The fourth way is to help make things simpler for the performer, which is a very appealing offer for almost anyone. (Slide 4 of 5)
	Slide 30 **Who's Responsible for Coachability?** - It's the performer's job to be coachable. - *However*, if you want to be a more effective coach, you will do what you can to help the performer feel more open to your coaching!	**Learning Content/Discussion** **Enhancing Coachability** To help solidify the learning on coachability, ask the participants this question: Is it really the coach's responsibility to increase the performer's coachability? Then present and discuss Slide 30. Ask participants to share some of their own experiences with techniques to enhance coachability. Encourage them to share both positive and negative examples. (Slide 5 of 5)
11:05 a.m. (10 min)	Slide 31 **Coachability Scenario 1** - Bob is frustrated with the pace of progress in the team, but it seems he is not sure what to do to help the team get unstuck. - From working with Bob, you know that he can get sidetracked when he feels overwhelmed, which can make him less coachable. - How might you help "Overwhelmed Bob" be more coachable?	**Learning Activity 5: Coachability Scenarios** This activity gives participants a chance to work together in small groups to define the concept of coachability and identify ideas to improve coachability back in their workplace. Take your time with this exercise because it will help cement the ideas you have just presented. Use instructions for the shorter version of this exercise in learning activity. Present scenario on the slide and then encourage groups to discuss the scenario and answer its question. Ask them to come up with at least three ways to improve the performer's coachability, one of which they are willing to share with the whole group.

TIMING	SLIDES	ACTIVITIES/NOTES/CONSIDERATIONS
11:15 a.m. (15 min)	Slide 32 Uncoachability Triggers - What are your coachability triggers? - Complete Assessment 2: Uncoachability Triggers Checklist. Check any trigger that has affected your coachability in the last month. - **How many did you check off?**	**Learning Activity 6: Uncoachability Triggers** - **Assessment 2: Uncoachability Triggers Checklist** Naturally we are coachable some of the time and uncoachable others. This short exercise will help participants build self-awareness of situations that tend to affect their coachability. If they can acknowledge their triggers, they can catch and prevent themselves from becoming uncoachable.
11:30 a.m. (5 min)	Slide 33 Key Distinction 5 The best coaching enabler, or lever, is coachability. If the performer is not open and ready, the coaching conversation is a waste of time. As a coach, job number one is to help enhance the performer's coachability. It's like proper hydration before and during a marathon. Without it, nothing else matters.	**Key Distinction 5** Share Key Distinction 5, which concerns the importance of coachability as a powerful coaching tool.
11:35 a.m. (45 min)	Slide 34 Lunch	**Lunch**
12:20 p.m. (15 min)	Slide 35 The Engine for Coaching Conversation Skills	**Learning Content/Lecture** **Conversation Skills: Creating Pull** Present the next quadrant of the model—conversation—the engine for coaching. (Slide 1 of 3)

TIMING	SLIDES	ACTIVITIES/NOTES/CONSIDERATIONS
	Slide 36 Conversation Skills - The first and most important part of conversation skills is **deep listening**, which we have already addressed. - The second most important conversation skill for coaches is **inquiry**. 　· Bottom line: Inquiry is asking questions to explore a topic. 　· Great inquiry creates pull. 　· To use inquiry, ask great questions.	**Learning Content/Lecture** **Conversation Skills: Creating Pull** For the conversation portion of the model there are two key behaviors: deep listening and inquiry. Participants practiced deep listening earlier in the workshop, so this section focuses on inquiry, which has two parts: creating pull and asking great questions. (Slide 2 of 3)
	Slide 37 Conversation Skills That Create Pull - Provide rallying cry that "rallies" - Are evocative—encourage reflection and bring out pride - Are provocative—excite, fascinate, and intrigue - Are memorable in some way - Make people feel great—bring out their awesomeness - Improve relationships and connection - Help people see the way forward and are catalytic - Provide advocacy—pave the way with some assistance	**Learning Content/Lecture** **Conversation Skills: Creating Pull** • **Handout 3: Conversation Characteristics That Create Pull** Spend at least 15 minutes on the conversation characteristics that create pull (Slide 37 and Handout 3). Share examples of each and ask participants for theirs. Create a robust discussion and you will see their "lightbulbs" go on. This will be especially true for managers, who will see how helpful these characteristics are for team discussions. (Slide 3 of 3)
12:35 p.m. (10-15 min)	Slide 38 Creating Pull - Using the Handout 3: Conversation Characteristics That Create Pull, brainstorm 10 ways you could increase pull in coaching conversations. - Be specific. Don't write: "Be Fascinating." Think of a few specific strategies you could use to increase fascination in a typical coaching discussion.	**Learning Activity 9: Creating Pull** • **Handout 3: Conversation Characteristics That Create Pull** This activity will help participants explore ways to increase performer engagement and ownership through techniques that use *pull* rather than *push* practices. To facilitate the exercise, follow instructions in the learning activity and refer participants to the slide. Debrief the activity with the group using discussion questions in the learning activity.

TIMING	SLIDES	ACTIVITIES/NOTES/CONSIDERATIONS
12:45 p.m. (5 min)	Slide 39 Key Distinction 6 Pull is better than push. This is particularly true with regards to coaching, but applies to most conversations. Pull adds the right kind of energy.	**Key Distinction 6** Finish this section on creating pull in conversations by going over Key Distinction 6. This foundational learning tends to really resonate with participants: Pull is better than push.
12:50 p.m. (15 min)	Slide 40 Ask Better Questions Use inquiry conversations when... - Performers are stuck and are not sure how to move forward. - Performers are learning new tasks or skills. - Performers are enthusiastic about a new idea or need your help to create a plan for how to approach their work. - Performers have only partial information or could benefit from another point of view.	**Learning Activity/Lecture** **Conversation Skills: Ask Better Questions** Coaching is either listening or asking questions, so it is important to help coaches ask better questions. Inquiry conversations are appropriate when performers have a goal or interest and express some commitment and ownership. (Slide 1 of 4)

	Slide 41
	
	Ask Better Questions
	
	- Broadly, questions fall into one of two categories:
	  - Closed-Ended: Yes, No, or number answer.
	  - Open-Ended: Require a more complete answer.
	- Great questions are open-ended and go beyond to provoke bigger thinking.
		Learning Activity/Lecture
		Conversation Skills: Ask Better Questions
		
		Cover the difference between closed and open-ended questions. Remind participants that great questions are open-ended and help the performer think bigger and better.
		
		Share examples of unhelpful questions, which are generally too narrow, obvious, or patronizing:
		• Do you want your team to listen to you?
		• Are you committed to do what it takes?
		• Are you comfortable with that?
		
		(Slide 2 of 4)

	Slide 42 Examples of Better Questions - What are your burning questions about this idea? - Would it help if we talked through your ideas and questions about this? - I don't want to get in the way of your creativity or inadvertently squash new ideas, so why don't you start by telling me where things stand and where you want to head with the plan, idea, or goal? - I can see that you have a lot of interest in and ownership for this project. Is there anything getting in your way?	**Learning Activity/Lecture** **Conversation Skills: Ask Better Questions** Use this slide to share examples of better questions. (Slide 3 of 4)

TIMING	SLIDES	ACTIVITIES/NOTES/CONSIDERATIONS
	Slide 43	**Learning Activity/Lecture**
		Conversation Skills: Ask Better Questions
	Pitfalls to Avoid Behaviors that help reduce discovery include - Over-sharing your story (think. "*This is not about me.*"). - Assigning value and judgment. - Cutting off conversation (poor listening). - Asking routine questions that don't challenge the performer. - Playing devil's advocate too much (becomes a conversation killer if overdone).	The most common coaching conversation pitfall is getting in the way of the performer's discovery. Have some fun discussing the pitfalls of inquiry. Most people will be able to relate to these behaviors, especially as performers.
1:05 p.m. (10-15 min)	Slide 44	**Learning Activity 10: Ask Better Questions**
		Conversation Skills: Ask Better Questions
	Ask Better Questions Activity - Imagine that you are coaching John, who is frustrated with the pace of progress on a project that means a lot to him. - In your group, brainstorm three GREAT questions that might help John explore his situation and make progress. (5 minutes)	Participants will practice using questions in the two coaching sessions today, so you won't need to conduct an in-depth exercise in this section. But you can give them a brief taste of crafting their own "better" questions. This activity will challenge coaches to brainstorm great questions in a specific coaching situation. Use the instructions in the learning activity to facilitate the exercise and lead the group debriefing discussion.
1:15 p.m. (5 min)	Slide 45	**Key Distinction 7**
		Coaches need to inspire and catalyze new thinking. They must ask great questions.
	Key Distinction 7 Be provocative. Ask great questions. Coaches need to inspire and catalyze new thinking.	
1:20 p.m. (30 min)	Slide 46	**Learning Activity 14: Getting Started and Asking Great Questions**
	First Practice: Getting Started and Asking Great Questions - Relax, this is going to be fun. No pressure at all. Really. - You and your partner will play both roles—performer and coach. - Circle one item on Handout 8: Getting Started Practice Worksheet that you'd like coaching on. - Swap worksheet your partner. Take 3 minutes to write down a few ideas for questions that will start the coaching discussion. - Begin coaching conversation: 1) determine the performer's goal, and 2) identify current barriers to success. (10 minutes each round; take your time!) - Enjoy the discussion: coaches listen deeply; performers be coachable. (Coaches: Listen more than you talk.)	• **Handout 8: Getting Started Practice Worksheet** This is the first of two practice coaching sessions. Do not cut this exercise short and make sure that participants don't speed through it and then talk to their partner about other things. If you have a large group, you might need a co-facilitator to monitor the room. Use the instructions in the learning activity to guide this coaching session.

TIMING	SLIDES	ACTIVITIES/NOTES/CONSIDERATIONS
1:50 p.m. (10 min)	Slide 47 Taming the "Meaning Making" Machine Perspective Skills	**Learning Content/Lecture** **Perspective Skills** Use this slide to transition to the next quadrant of the Coaching Model, which is perspective—taming the "meaning-making" machine. (Slide 1 of 4)
	Slide 48 Perspective Skills Defined - One of the most valuable coaching services you can provide is to help performers adopt a healthy and helpful perspective about their situation. - Perspective is most needed when performers feel overwhelmed, unsuccessful, stuck, hassled, unconfident, or unworthy. - Facilitating perspective requires critical, contextual, and systems thinking.	**Learning Content/Lecture** **Perspective Skills** This can be the toughest or the easiest section of the workshop to facilitate, depending on how you approach it. Here's the easy way: Help coaches see that often the most valuable thing they can do is help performers see their situations a bit differently. That's what the model means by perspective—the way people look at and evaluate their circumstances, challenges, or opportunities. Don't worry about spending too much time explaining it. Let the exercise in the next section do the heavy lifting to help participants understand how they can help performers improve their perspectives. (Slide 2 of 4)

	Slide 49
	
	Why Performers Lack Perspective
	
	- Performers might lack perspective if they
	   Are operating with incomplete information
	   Have a tendency to worry about things
	   Are living in victim mode or feeling overwhelmed, which is getting in their way of moving forward.
	- These challenges can alter the meaning performers assign to situations.
	- We are meaning-making machines!
		Learning Content/Lecture
		
		Perspective Skills
		
		Use Slide 49 to review the reasons why performers lack perspective.
		
		(Slide 3 of 4)

	Slide 50 How Coaches Can Help - Use critical thinking to help performers assess the situation. - Use systemic thinking to help performers see and consider connections and interdependencies. - Help performers put things in context. Nothing occurs in isolation; we work and progress in the environment.	**Learning Content/Lecture** **Perspective Skills** Use Slide 50 to review how coaches can help performers gain perspective. (Slide 4 of 4)

TIMING	SLIDES	ACTIVITIES/NOTES/CONSIDERATIONS
2:00 p.m. (15-20 min)	Slide 51 Quick Start to Critical Thinking Exercise • Use Handout 9: Quick Start to Critical Thinking Worksheet to practice helping a performer improve his or her perspective. • At the top of the worksheet, circle the problem or challenge you can most relate to in your work. • Swap sheets with your partner. Interview your partner using the questions on the worksheet (don't get caught up trying to identify unknown data). • Switch roles with your partner and repeat the exercise. © 2015 ATD. Used with permission. / SLIDE 051	**Learning Activity 15: Quick Start to Critical Thinking** • **Handout 9: Quick Start to Critical Thinking Worksheet** In this exercise, participants will practice using critical thinking questions in a coaching conversation, guided by Handout 9. The activity helps participants understand what the model means by perspective and what it looks like in practice. Follow instructions in the learning activity and on the slide to facilitate the activity. (Slide 1 of 2)
	Slide 52 Critical Thinking Exercise Debrief • As the coach, what did you notice about using the worksheet questions to "interview" the performer? How did the conversation go? • As the performer, how did it feel to be asked these questions? Did you notice any coachability triggers popping up? • How do you think this type of tool can help performers improve their perspective and, as a result, enhance focus, action, and progress? © 2015 ATD. Used with permission. / SLIDE 052	**Learning Activity 15: Quick Start to Critical Thinking** To test participants' understanding of the concepts of perspective and its relation to critical thinking, lead a discussion debriefing Learning Activity 15 using the discussion questions in the learning activity and on Slide 52. (Slide 2 of 2)
2:15 p.m. (5 min)	Slide 53 Key Distinction 8 Performers possess everything they need to solve their problems and make progress—but they sometimes lack perspective. © 2015 ATD. Used with permission. / SLIDE 053	**Key Distinction 8** Present Key Distinction 8. Coaches can help performers gain perspective and clarify the best ways forward to make progress.
2:20 p.m. (10 min)	Slide 54 Break © 2015 ATD.	**Break**

TIMING	SLIDES	ACTIVITIES/NOTES/CONSIDERATIONS
2:30 p.m. (10-15 min)	Slide 55 Intentions require progress to become accomplishments. Progress Skills	**Learning Content/Lecture** **Progress Skills** The final quadrant of the Coaching Model is progress—intentions require it to become accomplishments. For coaches, this can be a tricky part of coaching because if the performer owns the discussion, how can coaches help hold him or her accountable? This is a good question to explore because if ensuring progress is done poorly, it can turn into the reason performers disengage from the coaching. Take some time to go over the slides in this section, sharing your own examples. There is no exercise in this section because practicing the progress discussion is a big part of the final coaching session. (Slide 1 of 4)

	Slide 56
	
	Progress Skills
	· Many performers have vision but fail to produce satisfactory results because of inadequate progress.
	· Even in small amounts, progress is one of the most powerful motivators we can tap into.
	· Coaches help enable progress by
	  · Helping performers create a plan
	  · Managing agreements
	  · Inspiring action
		Learning Content/Lecture
		
		Progress Skills
		
		Define *progress* in coaching. It can be a powerful tool in the coaching toolkit. Review three ways that coaches can enable progress:
		
		• Helping performers create action plans
		
		• Managing agreements
		
		• Inspiring action.
		
		(Slide 2 of 4)

	Slide 57 Facilitating Progress with an Action Plan There are many ways to help performers create an action plan: · Not ideal: Ask them: "What are you going to do?" · Not ideal: Tell them: "You need to come up with an action plan." · Better: Help performers identify small actions that they are highly motivated to carry out and that are so simple they can easily begin to move forward.	**Learning Content/Lecture** **Progress Skills** There are many ways to help performers create action plans, but not all are ideal. Share examples on the slide of what works and what doesn't. (Slide 3 of 4)

TIMING	SLIDES	ACTIVITIES/NOTES/CONSIDERATIONS
	Slide 58 Questions to Facilitate Progress Progress	**Learning Content/Lecture** **Progress Skills** Lead a discussion of how to use great questions to help performers move forward on their action plans. (Slide 4 of 4)
2:40 p.m. (2 min)	Slide 59 Key Distinction 9 Progress is a powerful motivator. Coaching helps facilitate progress, and even the tiniest of steps forward fuels success.	**Key Distinction 9** Share Key Distinction 9 with participants to help solidify the idea of progress as a potent motivator in the coaching process.
2:42 p.m. (3 min)	Slide 60 Great Coaches Seek Coaching	**Learning Content/Lecture** **Seek Coaching** Let participants know that they have completed the review of the Coaching Model's four essential coaching skills: coachability, conversation, perspective, and progress. Now, to improve their skills in each of the four quadrants, they need to practice giving and receiving coaching. Put simply, great coaches seek coaching. Share these two techniques for seeking coaching: 1) be willing to go first and 2) be genuinely thankful. Review sample opening lines they can use to request coaching.

TIMING	SLIDES	ACTIVITIES/NOTES/CONSIDERATIONS
2:45 p.m. (55-60 min)	Slide 61 Final Practice Coaching Sessions You know this will be fun! You and your new partner will play both roles—performer and coach. Take 5 minutes to review Handout 2: Coaching Roles and then complete Handout 4: My Coaching Worksheet. Swap Handout 4 with your partner and then prepare for your role as coach using Handout 7: Practice 2 Coaching Worksheet. (15 minutes) Begin the coaching conversation (two rounds, with each person playing both coach and performer) (20 minutes each round; don't skimp!) Enjoy the discussion, listen deeply (coach), and be coachable (performer).	**Learning Activity 13: Final Practice Coaching Session** • **Handout 4: My Coaching Worksheet** • **Handout 7: Practice 2 Coaching Worksheet** • **Handout 2: Coaching Roles** This is the final practice session and should bring together everything the participants have learned. It requires them, as coaches, to listen deeply, create pull, ask great questions, improve coachability, provide perspective, and ensure performer progress—the complete Coaching Model. To facilitate this exercise, follow the instructions in the learning activity and refer participants to the slide. When you are processing this activity, ask participants how they feel about coaching now compared with before the workshop. Use debriefing questions from the learning activity to help lead the conversation.
3:40 p.m. (5 min)	Slide 62 Key Distinction 10 Coaching is a wonderful gift. If you believe in it—and seek it—you will be better at providing it. If you don't seek coaching, what message do you send to other performers?	**Key Distinction 10** Share the final Key Distinction—coaching is a gift. If you seek it, you will be better at providing it.
3:45 p.m. (5 min)	Slide 63 Wrap-Up and Review Performer's Role Conversation · Perspective Coachability · Progress Coach's Role	**Wrap-Up and Review** Because participants just completed the long practice session, the closing does not include action planning. Remind the participants of the journey they have gone through together to explore coaching. Start with the Coaching Model and its roles and essential coaching skills. (Slide 1 of 4)

TIMING	SLIDES	ACTIVITIES/NOTES/CONSIDERATIONS
	Slide 64	**Wrap-Up and Review**
	Workshop Objectives: How Did We Do? · Define what great coaching is and know what it looks like in practice. · Determine your role as a coach and the role of performer. · Learn a model of coaching and practice several key coaching skills. · Build your self-awareness as a coach and performer and increase your confidence and interest in coaching.	Review the objectives and ask participants how they think they did. (Slide 2 of 4)
	Slide 65	**Wrap-Up and Review**
	Coaching: Why We Love It · Coaching is a fabulous because it is 100-percent service. · A coaching conversation is a high-value-added activity well worth your effort. · Coaching can also be a bit mysterious because you might not know why some approaches work and others don't (and this might change from performer to performer).	Stoke their enthusiasm for great coaching as a very unique and helpful endeavor. (Slide 3 of 4)
	Slide 66	**Wrap-Up and Review**
	Being a coach is ... · A privilege · A joy—it feels great to help others grow · A burden—it's not easy coaching in the ways we have discussed during this workshop · The best way to maximize your impact on others	Assure them that anyone can learn to be a coach and that this workshop is a substantial start on their journey toward being great coaches. (Slide 4 of 4)
3:50 p.m. (5 min)	Slide 67	**Key Distinctions Roundup**
	Key Distinctions Roundup 1. Coaching helps performers make progress toward their goals and intentions. 2. Great coaches 'show up' based on what will best help the performer move forward. 3. Great coaches listen in ways that bring out the best in performers. 4. Successful performers are highly coachable; they ask for and welcome coaching. 5. The best coaching enabler, or lever, is coachability. 6. Pull is better than push. 7. Be provocative. Ask great questions. Coaches inspire and catalyze new thinking. 8. Performers possess everything they need to solve their problems and make progress—but they sometimes lack perspective. 9. Progress is a powerful motivator. Coaching helps facilitate progress, and even the tiniest of steps forward fuels success. 10. Coaching is a wonderful gift. If you believe in it—and seek it—you will be better at providing it.	This slide brings together all 10 Key Distinctions. Read them as a way of reviewing the most important beliefs about coaching. Ask participants which distinction will be most useful for them. Share the distinction that has most affected your own perspective about coaching and why.

TIMING	SLIDES	ACTIVITIES/NOTES/CONSIDERATIONS
3:55 p.m. (5 min) Ends 4:00 p.m.	Slide 68 **Next Steps** - Ask for coaching often. - Start offering more coaching. - Notice your coachability triggers and what causes others to be less open. - Explore the coaching skills that you feel are least developed and vigorously use your strengths to help others. © 2018 ATD. Used with permission. · SLIDE #104	**Closing and Next Steps** • **Handout 10: Workshop Evaluation Form** Close the workshop with a couple of suggestions about how to get more practice as a coach and performer. Share any final details and follow-up plans (highly recommended). See Chapters 10 and 11 for ideas to follow up the training with support and activities. Be open to answering any final questions on coaching or the concepts presented in the workshop. Conduct workshop evaluations. Remind participants that their insights help facilitators get better. Use Handout 10 or your own preferred form. (Slide 1 of 2)
	Slide 69 Thank you for your participation. Best of success! © 2018 ATD. Used with permission. · SLIDE #105	**Closing and Next Steps** And, finally, encourage participants to take a few moments to thank their peer coaches. That was real coaching—they should use it. Thank them for their participation and wish them best of success in their coaching! (Slide 2 of 2)

Key Points

- The overall objective of this one-day course is to provide a good introduction to coaching skills.

- The learning activities and practice sessions are designed to help participants feel more confident and comfortable initiating and navigating service-oriented coaching discussions.

- The course also explores how to help coaches be more receptive to coaching so that they can be more effective in the performer role.

What to Do Next

- Determine the schedule for training classes; reserve location and any catering you may wish to provide.

- Identify and invite participants.

- Inform participants about pre-work if you will be using it in the class.

- Review the workshop objectives, activities, and handouts to plan the content you will use.

- Prepare copies of the participant materials and any activity-related "extras." Refer to Chapter 15 for information on how to access and use the supplemental materials provided for this workshop.

- Gather any "fidgets" (quiet toys such as chenille stems, koosh balls, and so on) to place on the tables for your participants. See Chapter 8 for other ideas to enhance the learning environment of your workshop.

- If you will be co-facilitating with a partner, meet to agree on how you will split up the training parts and how you will support each other during exercises and transition points.

- Prepare yourself both emotionally and physically. Make sure you have taken care of any scheduling conflicts or personal challenges (as best you can), so that you can be fully present to facilitate the class.

- Get a good night's sleep before you facilitate your workshop so that you have the energy and focus to deliver a great class!

Chapter 3

Half-Day Coaching Workshop

What's in This Chapter

- Objectives of the half-day Coaching Workshop
- Background of the Coaching Model
- Summary chart for the flow of content and activities
- Half-day program agenda

This half-day Coaching Workshop will give participants a basic understanding of the Coaching Model and allow them to think through or practice several of its elements. This workshop is 25 percent lecture and 75 percent practice because the best way to learn how to coach is to either give or receive it. You will be spending most of the first hour presenting the Coaching Model in some detail, so make sure you serve coffee! Once the model review is complete, the rest of the workshop is interactive. The exercises start easy and progress to participants giving and receiving a complete coaching conversation.

The Backstory for the Coaching Model

The Coaching Model used for this course addresses the top needs of performers. It is not a linear or prescriptive process because a great coaching conversation always starts where the performer is (not the step in the coaching process where you left off last time). In some ways, this model might be more difficult for your training participants because it doesn't offer a simple eight-step list of things to do to be a better coach. Let's be clear; there is no eight-step list of things a coach can do to get better. Coaching is a service-oriented conversation and so must emerge from the needs of the performer.

If your training participants seem a bit unclear as to what they should "do" when coaching, reinforce the bottom line—do whatever will best help performers make progress and do it in a way that maintains the performers' ownership of their success.

Consider the example of two well-known brands to illustrate the fundamental belief upon which this coaching model is based. Ritz-Carlton hotels are renowned for their world-class service. When you stay at one of their hotels, you get what you need, when you need it, from professionals who make you feel great at every step in the service process. Now let's think about going to an Apple Store and signing up for an appointment with a Genius (Apple's term for its product experts). When it is your turn at the Genius Bar, you share your issue or question and the Genius tells you what's going on and how to solve your problem. At the Ritz-Carlton, the guest is the focus. At the Genius Bar, the Genius is. Our model of coaching should make performers feel more like they are staying at the Ritz-Carlton than sitting at the Genius Bar— high on customized service and low on advice. This is not to say that we don't all need a visit to our corporate Genius Bar every now and then—we do. But that's not what great coaching is about. In the introduction, coaching was described as a bespoke conversation. That's what Ritz-Carlton is known for: made-to-order service. And that's what your coaches will be known for after practicing these skills and methods.

A Note About the Presentation Slides and Facilitator's Notes

The presentation slides for this workshop have been designed based on two assumptions. The first assumption is that when you begin delivering this workshop, you will want all the help you can get! With this in mind, the presentation slides contain many verbal cues to help you facilitate the course well right from the start. The second assumption is that you will want to reduce the number of words or slides as you get more familiar with the course. When designing a course for others to facilitate, I always start with a slide deck that offers a lot of help, complete with full phrases or sentences (not just bullet points) so that you can convey the idea even before the material has become second nature to you. I expect that you will, in time, modify the slides to be less wordy.

Because the slides contain many verbal cues, the facilitator notes do not contain verbatim talking points, scripts, or transitions. After more than 30 years of delivering training, I know this to be true:

> Trainers who parrot talking points are not effective.

It is much better to use your own words and even fumble a bit than to use my words and sound like a robot. In addition, when you need to form the thought yourself, you "think" more about the content and how it applies to your audience.

Half-Day Workshop Objectives

By the end of the half-day workshop, participants will be able to

- Learn elements of the Coaching Model
- Determine their role as a coach and the role of the performer
- Practice creating effective coaching conversations.

Half-Day Workshop Overview

Here is a quick snapshot of the key sections and timing for the workshop. Print this page out and have it with you at the front of the classroom. Add a third column with your start time, end times, and milestones in between for easy reference and workshop pacing.

TOPICS	TIMING
Workshop Setup	60 minutes
Welcome and Introductions	10 minutes
Opener: My Coaching Story	10 minutes
What Is Coaching?	10 minutes
Coaching Model Overview	5 minutes
Coaching Roles: Coach and Performer	5 minutes
Coachability Skills	5 minutes
Conversation Skills	5 minutes
Perspective Skills	5 minutes
Progress Skills	5 minutes
Let's Practice	2 minutes
Learning Activity 4: Listen Deeply	18-20 minutes
BREAK	**10 minutes**
Learning Activity 6: Uncoachability Triggers/Assessment 2	15 minutes

Learning Activity 9: Creating Pull	15 minutes
Learning Activity 12: Critical Thinking Exercise	40 minutes
BREAK	**10 minutes**
Seek Coaching	5 minutes
Learning Activity 13: Final Practice Coaching Session	55-60 minutes
Wrap-Up and Review	5 minutes
Closing and Next Steps	5 minutes
TOTAL (without setup)	**240 minutes (4 hours)**

Half-Day Workshop Agenda

The detailed agenda that follows will be your guide to leading the course. Use it in conjunction with the facilitator instructions found in Chapter 12: Learning Activities.

Half Day: (8:00 a.m. to 12:00 p.m.)

TIME	SLIDES	TRAINING ACTIVITY AND NOTES
Before the Workshop (at least 60 minutes)		**Workshop Setup** Set up the room so that participants are seated in groups of 4 to 6 people. Ensure you have all your handouts copied and other supplies. Place sticky notes, pens, and markers in the middle of each table. Arrange for any food and beverages. It is nice to have a bowl of hard candy in the middle of each table. (You may want to include a sugar-free option as well.)
8:00 a.m. (10 min)	Slide 1 ATD Workshop Coaching Skills Half-Day Workshop	**Welcome and Introductions** Welcome everyone as they arrive. Briefly introduce yourself. (Slide 1 of 2)

TIME	SLIDES	TRAINING ACTIVITY AND NOTES
	Slide 2	**Welcome and Introductions**
	Workshop Objectives • Learn elements of the Coaching Model. • Determine your role as a coach and the role of the performer. • Practice creating effective coaching conversations.	Review the objectives for the workshop. Set the stage for it to be participative and immediately applicable when participants go back to their workplaces. If you have favorite ground rules that you use for other courses, feel free to share them here. Otherwise, go over basic expectations and logistics (restrooms, exits, no texting, and so on). (Slide 2 of 2)
8:10 a.m. (10 min)	Slide 3	**Opener: My Coaching Story**

	My Coaching Story
	
	Work in groups of 2 or 3 to answer the following:
	•Name, role
	•Your coaching story
	  • Experience: giving or receiving coaching, or your impression of coaching
	  • A goal you would like to discuss with a coach
		Use the prompts on the slide to conduct the opening icebreaker. Start by sharing a goal you would like to discuss with a coach so that you can establish the idea that everyone can and should seek coaching, even the highest performers.
		
		Then ask participants to discuss their answers to these prompts with the people at their table.
		
		Once you have given each group time to introduce themselves and discuss the prompts (about 10 minutes), ask participants to share a few examples of coaching goals with the whole group.

8:20 a.m. (10 min)	Slide 4	**Learning Content/Lecture** **What Is Coaching?**
	What Is Coaching?	Use this slide to begin the discussion of what we mean by coaching in this workshop. Many people are confused by the term *coaching*. Feel free to adjust these terms to fit your work culture. (Slide 1 of 3)
	Slide 5	**Learning Content/Lecture** **What Is Coaching?**
	Coaching... • Is a service-oriented discussion • Focuses on the performer's goals and interests • Can be one time or ongoing • Requires coach to "shape shift" to be most helpful • Requires the performer to lead the discussion and be coachable.	Present the basic definition of coaching we will be using in this workshop. Share that you will be introducing Key Distinctions throughout the course. These are the fundamental beliefs on which the workshop is built. (Slide 2 of 3)

TIME	SLIDES	TRAINING ACTIVITY AND NOTES
	Slide 6 Coaching: Why We Love It - Coaching is a fabulous because it is 100-percent service. - A coaching conversation is a high-value-added activity well worth your effort. - Coaching can also be a bit mysterious because you might not know why some approaches work and others don't (and this might change from performer to performer).	**Learning Content/Lecture** **What Is Coaching?** Share your enthusiasm for great coaching with your participants as a very unique and helpful endeavor. Assure them that anyone can learn to be a great coach. (Slide 3 of 3)
8:30 a.m. (5 min)	Slide 7 Coaching Model	**Learning Content/Lecture** **Coaching Model Overview** This segment of the workshop will begin the detailed review of the model. That said, move through the slides pretty quickly. The later exercises will help bring the more difficult concepts to life. (Slide 1 of 2)
	Slide 8 Coaching Model Performer's Role Conversation / Perspective Coachability / Progress Coach's Role	**Learning Content/Lecture** **Coaching Model Overview** • **Handout 1: Coaching Model** Introduce the Coaching Model (Handout 1) and share some initial thoughts on it. Great coaching is not about certification or following some prescribed process. Based on our definition, a prescribed process would not work because the performer might actually need something different than the process can give. So, the model here is both more difficult (checklists are easier) and less difficult (no set practices). It focuses on great coaching—those behaviors and practices that enable great coaches to make a big impact on performers and teams. (Slide 2 of 2)

TIME	SLIDES	TRAINING ACTIVITY AND NOTES
8:35 a.m. (5 min)	Slide 9 We are calling ourselves 'coaches' and 'performers' to emphasize the ownership role that those who receive coaching hold. Terms such as protégé and coachee emphasize the coach as expert. Coaching Roles	**Learning Content/Lecture** **Coaching Roles: Coach and Performer** • **Handout 2: Coaching Roles** Begin the review of the model with roles. Clarify that you will be calling the players *coaches* and *performers* rather than terms such as *protégé* or *coachee*. *Performer* places the emphasis in the right place—on the person receiving the coaching, not the coach. (Slide 1 of 4)

	Slide 10
	
	The Coach's Role
	· **Listen deeply; show interest.**
	· **Provide great service.**
	· Offer coaching; say "yes" to coaching.
	· Do what you can to help performers:
	  Clarify their goals, needs, and interests
	  Get unstuck
	  Make a connection
	  See the situation in a more beneficial way
	  Uncover alternative paths forward
	  Build self-awareness
	  Move forward
		Learning Content/Lecture
		Coach's Role
		
		Review the coach's role. The bolded items are the most important. The other attributes are nice and help, but service orientation and showing interest are the bottom line of coaching. If coaches only did these things, they would be successful.
		
		(Slide 2 of 4)

	Slide 11 The Performer's Role · **Be coachable.** · **Have a goal you want to work on.** · Seek coaching. Ask for the type of help you feel you need and be open to the idea that you might need something else entirely. · Let others influence you. Use the input and ideas you receive—consider it all even if you don't use it. · Own your progress. It is not the coach's job to motivate you or hold you accountable.	**Learning Content/Lecture** **Performer's Role** The purpose of learning the performer's role is two-fold. First, coaches need to recognize when coaching will and will not be effective. Second, all coaches are also performers, and they need to be open and coachable in that role as well. Review the performer's role requirements on slide. Items in bold type are the most important. (Slide 3 of 4)

TIME	SLIDES	TRAINING ACTIVITY AND NOTES
	Slide 12 The Performer's Role · In your previous coaching experiences, which aspect of the performer's role is modeled best (or worst)? · If a performer does not model his or her role well, should you offer coaching?	**Learning Content/Discussion** **Performer's Role** You don't want to let coaches off the hook for coaching even if the performer is not doing his or her part. Coaches should still be proactive and try. Lead a brief group discussion around questions on slide. Remind participants that if the performer does not pull into the discussion, even after the coach encourages him or her to open up, then maybe the time or circumstance is not right for coaching. (Slide 4 of 4)
8:40 a.m. (5 min)	Slide 13 The key to coaching is coachability. Coachability Skills	**Learning Content/Lecture** **Coachability Skills** Now that participants have a greater understanding about the two roles in the coaching model, move to the four key coaching skills: coachability, conversation, perspective, and progress. This next section drills down into coachability. (Slide 1 of 5)
	Slide 14 Coachability · Coachability is measured by how performers interact with their environment. · It is visible and observable behavior.	**Learning Content/Lecture** **Coachability Skills** Use the details on the slides in this section to ensure that participants understand the definition of the first of the essential coaching skills: coachability. It is important to clarify that coachability is not a permanent condition. People can change how open or closed to coaching they are in an instant. To help explain further, share an example: A speaker addressing a group of hospital leaders was being received very well until she showed she had not done her research of their industry and failed to tie her suggestion to their workplace reality (suggesting they let everyone work any hours they wanted in a busy, structured hospital setting). In that instant, the speaker turned off a number of participants and they became uncoachable. (Slide 2 of 5)

TIME	SLIDES	TRAINING ACTIVITY AND NOTES
	Slide 15 *What Coachability Looks Like* - Not defensive when challenged. - Welcomes feedback and ideas for improvement. - Asks for coaching. - Considers and uses ideas offered by others. - Seeks training and development in the form of reading, classes, new assignments, and coaching from others. - Has a good sense of his or her strengths and weaknesses. - Handles failures and setbacks with grace.	**Learning Content/Lecture** **Coachability Skills** *Coachability* may be a new term for some of your participants, so it can be very helpful to share what it looks like in practice. It is easy to spot if you know what to look for. (Slide 3 of 5)
	Slide 16 *What Uncoachability Looks Like* - Does not listen to ideas offered by others - Staunchly defends current ideas and approaches - Appears to be non-receptive or not interested in coaching - Does not engage in conversations about development and interprets suggestions to develop new skills as criticism - Is dismissive of others	**Learning Content/Lecture** **Coachability Skills** Now share what uncoachability looks like. There are so many things that affect whether a performer is coachable. Coaches can learn to observe uncoachability triggers in their performers and then create an environment that interests and engages them. (Note: We will do an exercise on triggers later.) (Slide 4 of 5)
	Slide 17 *Coachability Wrap-Up* - To provide the most effective coaching, take the initiative to help enhance the performer's coachability. - Coaching someone who is uncoachable is a waste of time and energy and can negatively affect the relationship.	**Learning Content/Discussion** **Coachability Skills** Emphasize that helping performers be more coachable is a core responsibility for coaches. In fact, it might be the most important thing they do. (Slide 5 of 5)
8:45 a.m. (5 min)	Slide 18 The Engine for Coaching Conversation Skills	**Learning Content/Lecture** **Conversation Skills** Transition discussion to the conversation quadrant of the model—the engine for coaching. (Slide 1 of 6)

TIME	SLIDES	TRAINING ACTIVITY AND NOTES
	Slide 19 Conversation Skills · The first and most important part of conversation skills is **deep listening**, which we have already addressed. · The second most important conversation skill for coaches is **inquiry**. 　· Bottom line: Inquiry is asking questions to explore a topic. 　· Great inquiry creates pull. 　· To use inquiry, ask great questions.	**Learning Content/Lecture** **Conversation Skills** The essential coaching skill of conversation includes two key behaviors: deep listening and inquiry. Discuss inquiry in this section and let participants know that they will get a chance to practice deep listening later in the workshop. (Slide 2 of 6)
	Slide 20 Ask Better Questions Use inquiry conversations when... · Performers are stuck and are not sure how to move forward. · Performers are learning new tasks or skills. · Performers are enthusiastic about a new idea or need your help to create a plan for how to approach their work. · Performers have only partial information or could benefit from another point of view.	**Learning Activity/Lecture** **Conversation Skills** Coaching is either listening or asking questions, so it is important to help coaches ask better questions. Inquiry conversations are appropriate when performers have a goal or interest and express some commitment and ownership. (Slide 3 of 6)
	Slide 21 Ask Better Questions · Broadly, questions fall into one of two categories: 　· Closed-Ended: Yes, No, or number answer. 　· Open-Ended: Require a more complete answer. · Great questions are open-ended and go beyond to provoke bigger thinking.	**Learning Activity/Lecture** **Conversation Skills** Participants will likely be familiar with the difference between closed and open-ended questions. Remind them that great questions are open ended and provoke bigger thinking. Share some examples of unhelpful questions, which are generally too narrow, obvious, or patronizing: • Do you want your team to listen to you? • Are you committed to do what it takes? • Are you comfortable with that? (Slide 4 of 6)
	Slide 22 Examples of Better Questions · What are your burning questions about this idea? · Would it help if we talked through your ideas and questions about this? · I don't want to get in the way of your creativity or inadvertently squash new ideas, so why don't you start by telling me where things stand and where you want to head with the plan, idea, or goal? · I can see that you have a lot of interest in and ownership for this project. Is there anything getting in your way?	**Learning Activity/Lecture** **Conversation Skills** Use this slide to share examples of better questions. (Slide 5 of 6)

TIME	SLIDES	TRAINING ACTIVITY AND NOTES
	Slide 23 Pitfalls to Avoid Behaviors that help reduce discovery include • Over-sharing your story (think: *This is not about me.*). • Assigning value and judgment. • Cutting off conversation (poor listening). • Asking routine questions that don't challenge the performer. • Playing devil's advocate too much (becomes a conversation killer if overdone).	**Learning Activity/Lecture** **Conversation Skills** The most common coaching conversation pitfall is getting in the way of the performer's discovery. Have some fun discussing the pitfalls of inquiry. Most people will be able to relate to these behaviors, especially as performers. (Slide 6 of 6)
8:50 a.m. (5 min)	Slide 24 Taming the "Meaning Making" Machine Perspective Skills	**Learning Content/Lecture** **Perspective Skills** Use this slide to transition to the next quadrant of the Coaching Model, which is perspective— taming the "meaning-making" machine. (Slide 1 of 4)
	Slide 25 Perspective Skills Defined • One of the most valuable coaching services you can provide is to help performers adopt a healthy and helpful perspective about their situation. • Perspective is most needed when performers feel overwhelmed, unsuccessful, stuck, hassled, unconfident, or unworthy. • Facilitating perspective requires critical, contextual, and systems thinking.	**Learning Content/Lecture** **Perspective Skills** This can be the toughest or the easiest section of the workshop to facilitate, depending on how you approach it. Here's the easy way: Help coaches see that often the most valuable thing they can do is help performers see their situations a bit differently. That's what the model means by perspective—the way people look at and evaluate their circumstances, challenges, or opportunities. Don't worry about spending too much time explaining it. Let the coaching practice session later in the workshop do the heavy lifting to help participants understand how they can help performers improve their perspectives. (Slide 2 of 4)

	Slide 26
	
	 Why Performers Lack Perspective
	
	 • Performers might lack perspective if they
	   Are operating with incomplete information
	   Have a tendency to worry about things
	   Are living in victim mode or feeling overwhelmed, which is getting in their way of moving forward.
	 • These challenges can alter the meaning performers assign to situations.
	 • We are meaning-making machines!
		Learning Content/Lecture
		 Perspective Skills
		
		 Use slide to review the reasons why performers often lack perspective.
		
		 (Slide 3 of 4)

TIME	SLIDES	TRAINING ACTIVITY AND NOTES
	Slide 27 How Coaches Can Help · Use critical thinking to help performers assess the situation. · Use systemic thinking to help performers see and consider connections and interdependencies. · Help performers put things in context. Nothing occurs in isolation; we work and progress in the environment.	**Learning Content/Lecture** **Perspective Skills** Use slide to review how coaches can help performers gain perspective. (Slide 4 of 4)
8:55 a.m. (5 min)	Slide 28 Intentions require progress to become accomplishments. Progress Skills	**Learning Content/Lecture** **Progress Skills** The final quadrant of the Coaching Model is progress—intentions require it to become accomplishments. For coaches, this can be a tricky part of coaching because if the performer owns the discussion, how can coaches help hold him or her accountable? This is a good question to explore because if ensuring progress is done poorly, it can turn into the reason performers disengage from the coaching. Take some time to go over the slides in this section, sharing your own examples. (Slide 1 of 5)

	Slide 29
	
	Progress Skills
	
	· Many performers have vision but fail to produce satisfactory results because of inadequate progress.
	· Even in small amounts, progress is one of the most powerful motivators we can tap into.
	· Coaches help enable progress by
	  · Helping performers create a plan
	  · Managing agreements
	  · Inspiring action
		Learning Content/Lecture
		Progress Skills
		
		Define *progress* in coaching. It can be a powerful tool in the coaching toolkit. Review three ways that coaches can enable progress:
		
		• Helping performers create action plans
		
		• Managing agreements
		
		• Inspiring action.
		
		(Slide 2 of 5)

TIME	SLIDES	TRAINING ACTIVITY AND NOTES
	Slide 30	**Learning Content/Lecture**
	Facilitating Progress with an Action Plan	**Progress Skills**
	There are many ways to help performers create an action plan:	There are many ways to help performers create action plans, but not all are ideal. Share examples on the slide of what works and what doesn't.
	· **Not ideal**: Ask them: "What are you going to do?" · **Not ideal**: Tell them: "You need to come up with an action plan." · **Better**: Help performers identify small actions that they are highly motivated to carry out and that are so simple they can easily begin to move forward.	(Slide 3 of 5)
	Slide 31	**Learning Content/Lecture**
	Questions to Facilitate Progress	**Progress Skills**
	Progress	Lead a discussion of how to use great questions to help performers move forward on their action plans.
		(Slide 4 of 5)
	Slide 32	**Learning Content/Lecture**
	Coaching Model Wrap-Up	**Coaching Model Wrap-Up**
	Our Coaching Model focuses on the essence of great coaching—those behaviors and practices that set apart coaches who make a big impact and those who don't.	Having covered the final essential coaching skill, briefly review the whole model once again. It explores two roles (coach and performer) and four essential coaching skills (coachability, conversation, perspective, and progress). Great coaching focuses on those behaviors and practices that make a big impact.
		(Slide 5 of 5)
9:00 a.m. (2 min)	Slide 33	**Let's Practice**
	Let's Practice!	Let participants know that you are shifting gears to the interactive portion of the workshop. Participants will be focusing their practice on a few of the most important aspects of coaching: listening deeply, uncoachability triggers, conversations that create pull, critical thinking skills, and an actual coaching session.

TIME	SLIDES	TRAINING ACTIVITY AND NOTES

9:02 a.m.
(18-20 min)
	Slide 34
	
	What Does It Mean to "Listen Deeply?"
	
	Let's give this a try:
	· Work in pairs or trios.
	· **Speakers:**
	  · Talk about a hobby that you love and why.
	· **Listeners:**
	  · Allow yourself to be totally engrossed in the speaker's story—just listen, be interested, be fascinated.
	  · Ask probing questions if the speaker stops talking. *Keep the speaker talking.*
	  · Don't interrupt the speaker. Don't start talking until the speaker has stopped. Allow a full 1-2 seconds in between the speaker's words and yours.
		Learning Activity 4: Listen Deeply
		
		This fun, interactive activity helps participants practice showing interest in others and giving others their full attention—in other words, deep listening. As a facilitator, make sure that you have given deep listening a try so you can share your personal experiences with the participants.
		
		Use this slide to help guide the exercise for the participants. The learning activity provides the full instructions for facilitation.
		
		(Slide 1 of 2)

	Slide 35 Deep Listening Debrief · What does it feel like to be listened to in this way? · What does it feel like to listen in this way? · Practice listening deeply every day. You will notice a big difference in how performers relate to you. They will be more engaged and take more ownership of their goals and next actions. · Deep listening can transform a conversation—really!	**Learning Activity 4: Listen Deeply** Use the processing questions on this slide to get a feel for whether the participants went deep enough in the activity. You might hear some say that deep listening feels intimate and perhaps uncomfortable in the workplace. Deep listening is intimate, so we want to be careful not to go to the point of being creepy or making people squirm. We do, however, want to show our undivided attention and interest, which is very uncommon in the workplace. Deep listening is the foundation of great coaching. (Slide 2 of 2)
9:20 a.m. (10 min)	Slide 36 Break	**Break**

TIME	SLIDES	TRAINING ACTIVITY AND NOTES
9:30 a.m. (15 min)	Slide 37 Uncoachability Triggers - What are your coachability triggers? - Complete Assessment 2: Uncoachability Triggers Checklist. Check any trigger that has affected your coachability in the last month. - **How many did you check off?**	**Learning Activity 6: Uncoachability Triggers** • **Assessment 2: Uncoachability Triggers Checklist** It is natural that we are coachable some of the time and uncoachable others. This short exercise will help participants build self-awareness of situations that tend to affect their coachability. If they can acknowledge their triggers, they can catch and prevent themselves from becoming uncoachable. Noticing triggers in themselves will also help them identify them in their performers.
9:45 a.m. (15 min)	Slide 38 Conversation Skills That Create Pull - Provide rallying cry that "rallies" - Are evocative—encourage reflection and bring out pride - Are provocative—excite, fascinate, and intrigue - Are memorable in some way - Make people feel great—bring out their awesomeness - Improve relationships and connection - Help people see the way forward and are catalytic - Provide advocacy—pave the way with some assistance	**Learning Activity 9: Creating Pull** • **Handout 3: Conversation Characteristics That Create Pull** This activity will help participants explore ways to increase performer engagement and ownership through techniques that use *pull* rather than *push* practices. As a lead-in to the activity, pass out the handout and review the conversation characteristics that create pull. You will see "lightbulbs" go on for your participants. This will be especially true for managers, who will see how helpful these characteristics are for team discussions. (Slide 1 of 2)
	Slide 39 Creating Pull - Using the Handout 3: Conversation Characteristics That Create Pull, brainstorm 10 ways you could increase pull in coaching conversations. - Be specific. Don't write: "Be Fascinating." Think of a few specific strategies you could use to increase fascination in a typical coaching discussion.	**Learning Activity 9: Creating Pull** • **Handout 3: Conversation Characteristics That Create Pull** To facilitate the exercise, follow instructions in the learning activity and refer participants to the slide. Debrief the activity with the group using discussion questions in the learning activity. (Slide 2 of 2)

TIME	SLIDES	TRAINING ACTIVITY AND NOTES
10:00 a.m. (40 min)	Slide 40 Critical Thinking Exercise · Let's use the Handout 6: Critical Thinking Worksheet to practice helping a performer improve his or her perspective. · At the top sheet, write a problem or challenge that you want to resolve or solve. · Switch worksheets with your partner. Take 10 minutes to interview your partner asking the questions on the worksheet (don't worry about identifying unknown data). · Switch roles and repeat the exercise.	**Learning Activity 12: Critical Thinking Exercise** • **Handout 6: Critical Thinking Worksheet** This exercise helps participants clarify what the model means by perspective and what it looks like in practice. Follow instructions in the learning activity to facilitate this exercise. (Slide 1 of 2)
	Slide 41 Critical Thinking Exercise Debrief As the coach, what did you notice about using the worksheet questions to "interview" the performer? How did the conversation go? As the performer, how did it feel to be asked these questions? Did you notice any coachability triggers popping up? How do you think this type of tool can help performers improve their perspective and, as a result, enhance focus, action, and progress?	**Learning Activity 12: Critical Thinking Exercise** To test participants' understanding of the concepts of perspective and its relation to critical thinking, lead a discussion debriefing Learning Activity 12 using the discussion questions in the learning activity and on the slide. (Slide 2 of 2)
10:40 a.m. (10 min)	Slide 42 Break	**Break**
10:50 a.m. (5 min)	Slide 43 Great Coaches Seek Coaching · Be willing to go first. Practice your opening lines: · "Will you help me make this better?" · "I'd love to get your thoughts on my approach to this and brainstorm potential paths forward." · "Play devil's advocate with me—what would the critics of this approach say and how could I win them over?" · "Thank you. I am always eager to hear how others might approach things." · "Can we take 10 minutes to dry run this?" · "I am feeling stuck and I am wondering if this is because I am not seeing something. Would you be open to exploring that with me?" · Be genuinely thankful. You will get great coaching and create a culture of coachability—a win-win.	**Learning Content/Content** **Seek Coaching** Put simply, great coaches seek coaching. Share these two techniques for seeking coaching: 1) be willing to go first, and 2) be genuinely thankful. Review sample opening lines they can use to request coaching. This discussion will help provide a lead-in to the practice coaching session.

TIME	SLIDES	TRAINING ACTIVITY AND NOTES
10:55 a.m. (55-60 min)	Slide 44 Final Practice Coaching Sessions You know this will be fun! You and your new partner will play both roles—performer and coach. Take 5 minutes to review Handout 2: Coaching Roles and then complete Handout 4: My Coaching Worksheet. Swap Handout 4 with your partner and then prepare for your role as coach using Handout 7: Practice 2 Coaching Worksheet. (15 minutes) Begin the coaching conversation (two rounds, with each person playing both coach and performer) (20 minutes each round; don't skimp!) Enjoy the discussion, listen deeply (coach), and be coachable (performer).	**Learning Activity 13: Final Practice Coaching Session** • **Handout 4: My Coaching Worksheet** • **Handout 7: Practice 2 Coaching Worksheet** • **Handout 2: Coaching Roles** This final practice session will bring together everything the participants have learned in the workshop. It requires them, as coaches, to listen deeply, create pull, ask great questions, improve coachability, provide perspective, and ensure performer progress—the complete Coaching Model. To facilitate this exercise, follow the instructions in the learning activity for the short version of the workshop. When you process this activity, ask participants how they feel about coaching now compared with before the workshop. Use debriefing questions from the learning activity to help lead the conversation.
11:50 a.m. (5 min)	Slide 45 Wrap-Up and Review Performer's Role Conversation	Perspective Coachability	Progress Coach's Role	**Wrap-Up and Review** Because participants just completed a long practice session, the closing does not need to include action planning. Remind the participants of the journey they have gone through together to explore coaching. Start with the Coaching Model and its roles and essential coaching skills. (Slide 1 of 5)
	Slide 46 Workshop Objectives: How Did We Do? - Learn elements of the Coaching Model. - Determine your role as a coach and the role of the performer. - Practice creating effective coaching conversations.	**Wrap-Up and Review** Review the objectives and ask participants how they think they did. (Slide 2 of 5)

TIME	SLIDES	TRAINING ACTIVITY AND NOTES
	Slide 47	**Wrap-Up and Review**
	Coaching . . . · Is a service-oriented discussion · Focuses on the performer's goals and interests · Can be one time or ongoing · Requires coach to "shape shift" to be most helpful · Requires the performer to lead the discussion and be coachable.	Revisit the definition of coaching developed during the course of the workshop. Encourage them to explore how their ideas about coaching have changed throughout the class. (Slide 3 of 5)
	Slide 48	**Wrap-Up and Review**
	Coaching: Why We Love It · Coaching is a fabulous because it is 100-percent service. · A coaching conversation is a high-value-added activity well worth your effort. · Coaching can also be a bit mysterious because you might not know why some approaches work and others don't (and this might change from performer to performer).	Stoke their enthusiasm for great coaching as a very unique and helpful endeavor. (Slide 4 of 5)
	Slide 49	**Wrap-Up and Review**
	Being a coach is ... · A privilege · A joy—it feels great to help others grow · A burden—it's not easy coaching in the ways we have discussed during this workshop · The best way to maximize your impact on others	Assure them that anyone can learn to be a coach and that this workshop is a substantial start on their journey toward being great coaches. (Slide 5 of 5)
11:55 a.m. (5 min) End 12:00 p.m.	Slide 50 Next Steps · Ask for coaching often. · Start offering more coaching. · Notice your coachability triggers and what causes others to be less open. · Explore the coaching skills that you feel are least developed and vigorously use your strengths to help others.	**Closing and Next Steps** • **Handout 10: Workshop Evaluation Form** Close the workshop with a couple of suggestions about how to get more practice as a coach and performer. Share any final details and follow-up plans (highly recommended). See Chapters 10 and 11 for ideas to follow up the training with support and activities. Be open to answering any final questions on coaching or the concepts presented in the workshop. Conduct workshop evaluations. Remind participants that their insights help facilitators get better. Use Handout 10 or your own preferred form. (Slide 1 of 2)

TIME	SLIDES	TRAINING ACTIVITY AND NOTES
	Slide 51 Thank you for your participation. Best of success! © 2010 ATD. Used with permission. | SLIDE #110	**Closing and Next Steps** And, finally, encourage participants to take a few moments to thank their peer coaches. That was real coaching—they should use it. Thank them for their participation and wish them best of success in their coaching! (Slide 2 of 2)

Key Points

- This half-day course provides a solid introduction to coaching.

- The learning activities and practice sessions are designed to help participants feel more confident and comfortable initiating and navigating service-oriented coaching discussions.

- The course also explores how to help coaches be more receptive to coaching so that they can be more effective in the performer role.

What to Do Next

- Determine the schedule for training classes; reserve location and any catering you may wish to provide.

- Identify and invite participants.

- Inform participants about pre-work if you will be using it in the class.

- Review the workshop objectives, activities, and handouts to plan the content you will use.

- Prepare copies of the participant materials and any activity-related "extras." Refer to Chapter 15 for information on how to access and use the supplemental materials provided for this workshop.

- Gather any "fidgets" (quiet toys such as chenille stems, koosh balls, and so on) to place on the tables for your participants. See Chapter 8 for other ideas to enhance the learning environment of your workshop.

- Prepare yourself both emotionally and physically. Make sure you have taken care of any scheduling conflicts or personal challenges (as best you can), so that you can be fully present to facilitate the class.

- Get a good night's sleep before you facilitate your workshop so that you have the energy and focus to deliver a great class!

Chapter 4
Customizing the Coaching Training Workshop

What's in This Chapter

- How to match your context to your intentions

- Ideas for customization, including shorter sessions, alternative four-hour sessions, options for pre-work and homework, and more

Your Invitation to Deviate!

These coaching workshops will work well as designed. They will also work well delivered in many other ways. Because coaching is a conversational skill, as long as you engage your participants in great conversations about coaching conversations, you can't go wrong. Well, you could go wrong if you stripped out all the practice and turned the workshop into the eight steps to coaching. But I know you won't do that.

Match Context to Your Intentions

I heard leadership author Peter Block say during a conference keynote presentation that "the context must match your intentions," and I think this is an important concept to explore here. Block shared a story about how he had been hired by the CEO of a large corporation to speak to 700 of his top leaders about empowerment. The CEO introduced Block to the theatre of blue-suited leaders who then clapped as Block walked up to the podium. It was in that moment, Block recalled, that he could tell something was wrong. The entire structure of the session was set up to reinforce hierarchy and discourage participation, but the topic was *empowerment!*

What does this mean relative to teaching coaching skills? Coaching occurs in conversations, so the training must be conversational. Also, our Coaching Model reinforces that performers must own their learning and so too must the participants in your workshop. They are coaches, but they are also the performers in the context of this course. So, as long as you ensure that you generate great conversations that pull the participants in, you are good to go rogue and make the workshop your own.

Ideas for Customization

When I conduct training that was created by someone else, I make a lot of changes, and I expect that you will do the same. Some changes are obvious, such as including language that is specific to your organization or industry. In addition to that, you might want to change the timing and focus of the sessions. Here are a few ideas that might fuel your creativity.

Shorter Sessions

You can deliver the two-day workshop in small chunks. I have worked with organizations that held monthly meetings where they offered one or two hours of training. When you chop up a class, however, you need to add time to your overall delivery. For example, you will likely need five two-hour sessions to accomplish the same learning outcomes as a two-day class because you need to add an introduction, conclusion, discussion of homework or pre-work, and reminders about previous and future sessions into each workshop.

If you would like to conduct the two-day workshop in shorter increments, Table 4-1 provides a breakdown of how I would do it.

These shorter training sessions provide a nice series based on the Coaching Model elements. But make sure that you put in all the connective tissue that will ensure learning is not lost between sessions. Start each session reviewing the last one and talking about the homework. Share the journey of the overall series of workshops so that participants will know what they will be learning. Remember to keep the vibe of the workshop informal and conversational.

Table 4-1: Two-Day Workshop in Five Sessions

SESSION	ACTIVITIES/CONTENT
Session 1: Coaching Roles	• Learning Activity 1: My Coaching Story • What Is Coaching? • Learning Activity 3: Coaching Skills Diagnostic/Assessment 1 • Coaching Roles • Learning Activity 4: Listen Deeply • Homework: Practice deep listening for 10 minutes each day.
Session 2: Coachability Skills	• Coachability Skills • Learning Activity 5: Coachability Scenarios • Learning Activity 6: Uncoachability Triggers • Starting the Coaching Conversation • Learning Activity 7: Ways to Offer Coaching • Homework: Notice how coachability and uncoachability show up for you and others; start one coaching conversation with someone you know well (so it's safe).
Session 3: Conversation Skills	• Learning Activity 9: Creating Pull • Learning Activity 10: Ask Better Questions • Learning Activity 11: First Practice Coaching Session • Homework: Ask one great question at every meeting you attend and watch what happens; focus on creating more PULL throughout your day (not just when coaching).
Session 4: Perspective and Progress Skills	• Perspective Skills • Learning Activity 12: Critical Thinking Exercise (expand this) • Progress Skills (add an activity to help participants create action plans) • Homework: Use questions on Handout 6: Critical Thinking Worksheet to help a team member.
Session 5: Practice Coaching	• Learning Activity 13: Final Practice Coaching Session • Revisit Assessment 1: Coaching Skills Diagnostic. Lead a discussion around this question: Do participants feel they have improved their coaching skills? • Transition to follow-up learning plan.

Alternative Four-Hour Workshops

Many organizations like the four-hour workshop format because it allows participants to check in on their jobs and still attend the training. The four-hour workshop in this book focuses on listening, coachability, and critical thinking but feel free to make some changes. I recommend that you keep the emphasis on listening because it tends to be one of the primary weaknesses for coaches (or leaders!). Also, I am a firm believer in the importance of coachability. That said, if you think that your participants would benefit most from spending more time practicing inquiry, that would be an effective addition to a four-hour workshop (start with overall model review, perhaps the listening exercise, then inquiry). And if you want to expand the conversation characteristics that create *pull*, a four-hour session would also work well (the characteristics that create *pull* tend to resonate with participants). Whatever you do, do not remove the practice session. This is the most important part of the four-hour class. You may, however, need to modify the practice exercise to better line up with the new focus of the workshop.

Options for Pre-Work and Homework

I am a huge fan of pre-work and homework because the more you can get participants to reflect on and engage with the material, the better. I don't expect everyone in the workshop to do the pre-work or homework, but the more interesting it is, the more likely they will be to complete it (reference conversation characteristics that create *pull* here). Pre-work must be as fascinating, interesting, memorable, and as fun as possible. Here are my favorite sources for pre-work:

- Short blog posts or online articles from the top thinkers in the field (should be short—no more than 10 minutes to read)

- Online video clips (TED.com is a favorite source)

- Two or three great questions (make them provocative or evocative)

- Short video message recorded by facilitator about the workshop (what to start thinking about)

- Two- to four-question survey to help facilitator better understand how participants feel about the topic and their experiences

- Quick webinar as a prelude (record it and then email the link for those who cannot attend).

For homework, I like to ask participants to practice something they have learned in the workshop. Whatever the practice is, it should be something small and doable. You can ask them, for example, to listen deeply for at least 5 minutes each day. This is an ideal approach to homework when you have multiple meeting days in a learning series.

Other Ideas

Teams: There are several activities offered in this book that you can use or modify for team learning so that they can practice more peer coaching. For example, nearly all the pairs activities would work well in a team meeting (you would pair people up there, too). In particular, you might want to use Learning Activity 12: Critical Thinking Exercise in a team setting. All these ideas assume that you have shared the overall Coaching Model at some point so participants know how to put the topic into context.

Blended Learning. If you need to shorten the workshop, you can do the initial model review by webinar and leave all the activities for the in-class workshop. This would save you about two hours of in-class workshop time. You could also use a webinar format with pairs activities through teleconference during the webinar (I have done this with global organizations, and it works well). After presenting the content, break for a practice session that participants do with a partner over the telephone or Skype. After the practice session, participants come back to the webinar where you can help them process the activity. Keep in mind that this approach is too hard to manage for groups of more than 30 people because keeping track of too many pairings is too difficult. I do not advocate using virtual or web-based training for coaching skills for very large audiences (100 or more), but you can do the model review this way and then break the group into smaller in-person workshops of 30 or fewer people.

The Bare Minimum

With any of these customization options, always keep in mind the essentials of training design (Chapter 6) and delivery (Chapter 8). At a bare minimum, remember to

- **Make It Fun.** Going back to Block's idea that the context needs to match our intentions, coaching is a topic that is all about creating *pull*. You can't push good coaching techniques on participants because they must be interested and engaged in becoming a great coach. The burden to have more pull in the classroom makes it a bit harder for trainers in terms of design and time management but also easier in terms of participant engagement and enjoyment. Pull is more fun, so coaching training ought to be fun too.

- **Prepare, Prepare, Prepare.** Ready the room, the handouts, the equipment, and you. Familiarize yourself with the content, materials, and equipment. Practice can only make you a better facilitator. The more comfortable you feel, the more open and relaxed you will be for your participants.

- **Start Well.** The beginning of a session is a crucial time in the workshop dynamic. How the participants respond to you, the facilitator, can set the mood for the remainder of the workshop. Get to the classroom at least 30 to 60 minutes before the session is to begin. Be ready to welcome the participants, not deal with problems; be free and available to them. Ask them simple questions while they are settling to start building rapport. After introducing yourself, provide an activity in which participants can meet each other. The more time they spend getting to know each other, the more all of you will benefit as the session begins.

- **Don't Lecture Too Long!** Adult learners like to have fun and participate in interactive learning opportunities. Be sure to vary the learning and teaching method regularly (recommended every 10-15 minutes) to keep the pace active and engaging.

- **End Strong.** Providing time for participants to reflect and create an action plan at the end of a module or session will help solidify learning. Don't skip this opportunity to encourage participants to take action on something they have learned.

What to Do Next

- When customizing a workshop, it is important to have a clear understanding of the learning objectives. Conduct a needs analysis to identify the gap between what the organization needs and what the employees are able to do and then determine how best to bridge that gap. At the minimum, you should identify who wants the training, how the results will be defined, why the training is being requested now, and what the budget is. Chapter 5 provides more guidance on identifying training needs.

- Modify or add your own content to an existing agenda from Chapters 1-3 or create your own agenda using the learning support documents included in this volume. There is no one way to flow coaching content, but you must ensure that the topics build on one another and that you solidly connect the concepts and ideas together to leverage the most of the learning opportunity.

- Make sure to incorporate interactive practice activities into the design of the workshop.

- Compile and review all learning activities, handouts, and slides you will use for the session.

- Build a detailed plan for preparing for this session, including scheduling and room reservations, invitations, supply list, teaching notes, and time estimates.

SECTION II

ESSENTIALS OF EFFECTIVE COACHING TRAINING

Chapter 5

Identifying Needs for Coaching Training

What's in This Chapter

- Discovering the purpose of needs analysis
- Introducing some data-gathering methods
- Determining the bare minimum needed to deliver training

Ideally, you should always carry out a needs analysis before designing and creating a workshop to address a performance gap. The cost of *not* identifying and carefully considering the performance requirement can be high: wasted training dollars, unhappy staff going to boring or useless sessions, increased disengagement of employees, and so forth. But the world of training is rarely ideal, and the existence of this book, which essentially provides a workshop in a box, is testament to that. This chapter describes the essential theory and techniques for a complete needs analysis to provide the fundamentals of the process and how it fits into designing learning. However, because the decision to train may already be out of your hands, the last part of this chapter provides a bare-bones list of things you need to know to train effectively even if someone just handed you this book and told you to put on a workshop.

Why Needs Analysis?

In short, as a trainer, learning professional, performance consultant, or whatever job title you hold, your role is to ensure that the employees of your organization know how to do the work that will make the organization succeed. That means you must first identify the skills, knowledge, and abilities that the employees need for optimal performance and then determine where these are lacking in the employee population to bridge that gap. However, the most important reason for needs assessment is that it is not your learning experience. You may deliver it, but the learning belongs to the learner. Making decisions for learners about what performance they need without working with them is inappropriate. If you are an experienced facilitator, you have a large repository of PowerPoint decks at your disposal. Resist the urge while talking with your customers to listen for words that allow you to just grab what you already have. Be open to the possibilities. A training needs analysis helps you do this (see Figure 5-1). Methods to identify this information include strategic needs analysis, structured interviews, focus groups, and surveys.

Strategic Needs Analysis

An analysis of future directions usually identifies emerging issues and trends with a major potential effect on a business and its customers during a two- to three-year period. The analysis helps a business develop goals and programs that proactively anticipate and position the organization to influence the future.

To conduct such an analysis, organizations look at issues such as expected changes within the business (for example, technology and professional requirements) and expected changes outside the company (for example, the economy, demographics, politics, and the environment).

Figure 5-1. Introducing the ADDIE Model

A needs analysis is the first step in the classic instructional design model called ADDIE, which is named after its steps: analysis, design, development, implementation, and evaluation. Roughly speaking, the tasks involved in ADDIE are

1. **Analysis:** Gather data about organizational and individual needs as well as the gap between the goals the organization means to accomplish and the skills and knowledge needed to accomplish those goals.

2. **Design:** Identify and plan the topics and sequence of learning to accomplish the desired learning.

3. **Development:** Create the components of the learning event, such as learning activities and materials.

4. **Implementation:** Put on the learning event or launch the learning materials.

5. **Evaluation:** Gather data to determine the outcome of the learning to improve future iterations of the learning, enhance materials and facilitation, and justify budget decisions.

Instructional design models such as ADDIE are a systematic approach to developing learning and could also be viewed as a project management framework for the project phases involved in creating learning events.

A Note from the Author: Needs Assessment for Coaching

When it comes to coaching skills, a needs assessment will help you 1) ensure that the organization really wants coaching training, 2) identify which coaching skills are most in need of development, and 3) determine whether training is the solution to the performance gap. *Coaching* is a term that leaders toss about like *communication* and *teamwork*. And as is the case for all of these terms, it is important to distinguish what behaviors the leaders are looking for and then determine if coaching skills training can help fill the need. Leaders will commonly say they want more coaching when they are really looking to improve employee accountability or engagement. Building accountability and engagement requires different skills than those associated with coaching (although coaching might have an indirect effect on these goals).

It is also important to make sure that gaps in performance can actually be filled with training. I once taught a coaching skills class for HR professionals of a Fortune 50 company. This company contacted me and asked for a coaching skills class, which they helped to create and even approved the learning objectives. When I taught the workshop, however, the participants told me that the content was interesting but that they would never use it because their jobs were set up such that they'd never have time to coach their internal clients. What a waste!

Results of an analysis provide a rationale for developing company and departmental goals and for making policy and budgetary decisions. From the analysis comes a summary of key change dynamics that will affect the business.

These questions often are asked in strategic needs analysis:

- What information did previous organizational analyses impart?
- Are those issues and trends still relevant?
- Do the results point to what may need to be done differently in the future?
- How has the organization performed in achieving results?
- What is the present workforce like?
- How will it change or need to change?
- What does the organization know about future changes in customer needs?
- Are customer surveys conducted, and if so, what do they reveal?
- How might the organization have to change to serve customers better?

- Is the company's organizational structure working to achieve results?
- What are the strengths and limitations of the company?
- What are the opportunities for positive change?
- What do competitors do or say that might have implications for the organization?
- What are the most important opportunities for the future?
- What are the biggest problems?
- Is the organization in a competitive marketplace?
- How does the organization compare with competitors?

The results can be summarized in a SWOT analysis model (strengths, weaknesses, opportunities, threats—see Figure 5-2). Action plans are then developed to increase the strengths, overcome the weaknesses, plan for the opportunities, and decrease the threats.

Structured Interviews

Start structured interviews as high up in the organization as you can go, with the CEO if possible. Make sure that you include input from human resource personnel and line or operations

Figure 5-2. SWOT Analysis Model

	STRENGTHS	WEAKNESSES
INTERNAL		
	OPPORTUNITIES	THREATS
EXTERNAL		

managers and supervisors. Managers and supervisors will want to tell you what they have seen and what they consider the most pressing issues in the organization.

Focus Groups

Focus groups can be set up to give people opportunities to brainstorm ideas about issues in the organization and to realize the potential of team involvement. One comment may spark another and so on. Focus groups should begin with questions that you prepare. It is important to record the responses and comments on a flipchart so everyone can see them. If that is not possible, you may simply take notes. Results of the sessions should be compiled.

Surveys

Surveys, whether paper- or web-based, gather information from a large or geographically dispersed group of employees. The advantages of surveys are speed of data collection, objectivity, repeatability, and ease of analysis.

Individual Learning Needs Analysis

While identifying organizational learning needs is critical to making the best use of an organization's training budget, analyzing individual learning needs is also important. Understanding the training group's current skills and knowledge can help to focus the training on those areas that require most work—this also helps to avoid going over what the individuals already know, thus wasting their time, or losing them by jumping in at too advanced a level. In addition, individual learning needs analysis can uncover unfavorable attitudes about training that trainers will be better able to address if they are prepared for them. For example, some learners may see the training as a waste of time, as an interruption to their normal work, or as a sign of potentially frightening organizational change.

Many of the same methods used to gather data for organizational learning needs are used for individual learning needs analysis. Analyzing employee learning needs should be carried out in a thoughtful, sensitive, and inclusive manner. Here are potential pitfalls to avoid:

- **Don't analyze needs you can't meet.** Training needs analysis raises expectations. It sends a message to employees that the organization expects them to be competent in particular areas.

- **Involve employees directly.** Sometimes employees don't see a value in participating in training. In assessing needs, trainers need to prepare employees to buy into the training. Asking useful questions and listening carefully to stated needs are excellent methods for accomplishing both of those goals. Ask these questions: "To what degree would you like to learn how to do [X] more effectively?" and "To what degree would you seriously consider participating in training to improve your competency in [X]?"

- **Make the identified needs an obvious part of your training design.** Trainees should be able to see that they have influenced the content and emphasis of the training session. A good practice is briefly to summarize the local trends discovered in the training needs analysis when you introduce the goals of the session.

- **Don't think of training as a "magic bullet."** Sometimes a given employee needs coaching, counseling, or consulting, which is best carried out one on one and customized to the individual and the situation. Still other times, the problem is caused by equipment or processes that need upgrading, not people who need training.

The Bare Minimum

As noted, in an ideal world, you would have gathered all this data about the needs of the organization and the employees and determined that training was the right way to connect those dots. However, even if the decision to put on this workshop has already been made, you still need a bare minimum of information to be successful:

- **Who is your project sponsor (who wants to do this, provides the budget, and so on)?** In fact, if you don't have a project sponsor, *stop* the project. Lack of a project sponsor indicates that the project isn't important to the business. Optimally, the project sponsor should come from the business side of the organization. If the project sponsor is the head of training, then the mentality behind the training—"build it and they will come"—is likely wrong. Even compliance training should have a functional sponsor.

- **What does the sponsor want the learners to be able to do when they are done with training?** How does the sponsor define measures of success? Answering these critical questions brings clarity to the sponsor's expectations and thus to the workshop design.

- **What are the objectives of the training?** Use the guideline ABCD to prepare objectives: identify the Audience, describe the Behavior (what will they be able to do that they can't do now), describe the Condition (what are the circumstances under which they need to be able to do the task; for example, will they have a job aid), and then specify to what Degree (level of quality).

- **Why does the sponsor want this right now?** Is something going on in the organization of which you should be aware?

- **What is the budget?** How much time and money will be invested in the training?

Key Points

- Needs analysis identifies the gap between what the organization needs and what the employees are able to do and then determines how best to bridge that gap.

- Methods of data gathering for needs analysis include strategic needs analysis, structured interviews, surveys, focus groups, and others.

- Sometimes, needs analysis is not an option, but some minimum information is necessary, including who wants the training, how the results will be defined, why the training is being requested now, and what the budget is.

What to Do Next

- If you have the option, carry out a needs analysis to determine if this training is really what your organization requires to succeed. If it isn't, prepare to argue against wasting time, money, and effort on training that will not support the organization's goals.

- If you don't have the option of a needs analysis, make sure that you seek out at least the bare minimum information to conduct effective training.

- Prepare the learning objectives using ABCD (identifying audience, behavior, condition, and degree).

- If you have little training background, read the next chapter (Chapter 6) to learn about the theories and concepts that are at the root of training design. If you are an experienced trainer, skim Chapter 6 on design theory or go straight to Chapters 7 and 8 for tips on leveraging technology and delivering training, respectively.

Additional Resources

Biech, E., ed. (2008). *ASTD Handbook for Workplace Learning Professionals.* Alexandria, VA: ASTD Press.

Biech, E., ed. (2014). *ASTD Handbook: The Definitive Reference for Training & Development.* Alexandria, VA: ASTD Press.

Russo, C. "Be a Better Needs Analyst." ASTD *Infoline* no. 258502. Alexandria, VA: ASTD Press.

Tobey, D. (2005). *Needs Assessment Basics.* Alexandria, VA: ASTD Press.

Chapter 6

Understanding the Foundations of Training Design

What's in This Chapter

- Introducing adult learning theory
- Exploring multiple intelligences
- Incorporating whole brain learning
- Learning how theory enters into practice

Because this book provides a fully designed workshop, you don't need to know all the details of designing a course—the design has already been done for you. However, understanding some of the principle design and learning theories that underpin this workshop is useful and helpful—especially if you are somewhat new to the field of workplace training and development. To effectively deliver training to learners requires a core understanding of how and why people learn. This gives you the flexibility to adapt a course to the unique learners in the room as needed.

When designing a coaching workshop, paying attention to content flow is especially important. While there is no one right way to flow coaching training content, you must ensure that the topics build on one another and that you solidly connect the concepts and ideas together so you leverage the most of the learning opportunity. Great coaching skills require practice, so always include interactive practice sessions in the design of the workshop. Short but well-designed activities can have significant impact.

Basic Adult Learning Theory

The individual trainee addressed in these workshops is typically an adult with learning needs that differ in many (but not all) ways from children. Much has been documented about how adults learn best. A key figure in adult education is Malcolm Knowles, who is often regarded as the father of adult learning. Knowles made several contributions to the field but is best known for popularizing the term *andragogy*, which refers to the art and science of teaching adults. Here are six assumptions about adult learners noted in *The Adult Learner: A Neglected Species* (1984):

- Adults need to know why learning something is important before they learn it.
- Adults have a concept of self and do not like others imposing their will on them.
- Adults have a wealth of knowledge and experience and want that knowledge to be recognized.
- Adults open up to learning when they think that the learning will help them with real problems.
- Adults want to know how the learning will help them in their personal lives.
- Adults respond to external motivations, such as the prospect of a promotion or an increase in salary.

Given these principles of adult learning, designing sessions that are highly interactive and engaging is critical (see sidebar for more tips). Forcing anyone to learn anything is impossible, so the goal of effective training design is to provide every opportunity and encouragement to the potential learner. Involvement of the learner is the key. As an old Chinese proverb says, "Tell me and I will forget. Show me and I may remember. Involve me and I will understand." The designs in this book use several methods to convey information and engage participants. By incorporating varied training media—such as presentation media, discussion sessions, small-group work, structured exercises, and self-assessments—these designs maximize active participant involvement and offer something for every learning style.

Tips for Adult Learning

To reach adult learners, incorporate these ideas into your next training session:

- Incorporate self-directed learning activities in the session design.
- Avoid overuse of lectures and "talking to." Emphasize discussion.
- Use interactive methods such as case studies, role playing, and so forth.
- Make the content and materials closely fit assessed needs.
- Allow plenty of time to "process" the learning activities.
- Include applications planning in each learning activity.
- Promote inquiry into problems and affirm the experience of participants.
- Give participants a rationale for becoming involved and provide opportunities for success.
- Promote getting acquainted and interpersonal linkages.
- Diagnose and prioritize learning needs and preferences before and during the session.
- Use learning groups as "home bases" for participants.
- Include interpersonal feedback exercises and opportunities to experiment.
- Use subgroups to provide safety and readiness to engage in open interchange.
- Make all learner assessment self-directed.
- Provide activities that focus on cognitive, affective, and behavioral change.

In addition to engaging the interest of the learner, interactive training allows you to tap into another source of learning content: the participants themselves. In a group-learning situation, a good learning environment encourages participants to share with others in the group so the entire group's cumulative knowledge can be used.

More Theoretical Ideas Important to Learning

Research on how people learn and how the brain works occurs continuously. A few ideas that come up frequently in training design and delivery are multiple intelligences and whole brain learning.

Multiple Intelligences

Multiple intelligences reflect how people prefer to process information. Howard Gardner, from Harvard University, has been challenging the basic beliefs about intelligence since the early 1980s. Gardner initially described a list of seven intelligences. In 1987, he added three additional intelligences to his list, and he expects the list to continue to grow. The intelligences are

- **interpersonal:** aptitude for working with others
- **logical/mathematical:** aptitude for math, logic, deduction
- **spatial/visual:** aptitude for picturing, seeing
- **musical:** aptitude for musical expression
- **linguistic/verbal:** aptitude for the written and spoken word
- **intrapersonal:** aptitude for working alone
- **bodily kinesthetic:** aptitude for being physical
- **emotional:** aptitude for identifying emotion
- **naturalist:** aptitude for being with nature
- **existential:** aptitude for understanding one's purpose.

A Note from the Author: Adult Learning Considerations for Coaching

Coaching can bring out the best and worst in performers. It's true! Many of the adult learning theory considerations referenced in this chapter are doubly true when facilitating coaching training. When it comes to coaching, for example, two-way communication, reflection, and sharing experiences are critical. Coaching is a social act, and so learning how to provide coaching is conversational. In addition, learning how to coach others can be intimidating, so making the practice sessions feel safe and supportive is critical. You will notice that the practices within the workshops build in length and complexity and set participants up for success.

One of the challenges that you may face is that some adult learners don't like role-playing activities. They will say they don't like these types of exercises but often it is more accurate to say they find role playing scary and uncomfortable because it requires them to perform a skill they have not had time to practice. The workshops in this book don't use role play, but they do use gradual real coaching sessions. There is nothing made up about the practices, and they are structured to reduce fear and resistance.

How do multiple intelligences affect your learning? Gardner believes that most people are comfortable in three or four of these intelligences and avoid the others. For example, if you are not comfortable working with other people, doing group case studies may interfere with your ability to process new material. Video-based instruction will not be good for people with lower spatial/visual aptitudes. People with strong bodily/kinesthetic aptitudes prefer to move around while they are learning.

Allowing your learners to use their own strengths and weaknesses helps them process and learn. Here's an example: Suppose you are debriefing one of the exercises in the material. The exercise has been highly interpersonal (team activity), linguistic (lots of talking), spatial/visual (the participants built an object), musical (music was playing), logical/mathematical (there were rules and structure), and kinesthetic (people moved around). You've honored all the processing styles except intrapersonal, so the people who process information in this manner probably need a return to their strength of working alone. Start the debriefing by asking people to quietly work on their own, writing down five observations of the activity. Then ask them to share as a group.

Whole Brain Learning

Ned Herrmann pioneered the concept of whole brain learning in the 1970s, developing the Herrmann Whole Brain Model, which divides the brain into four distinct types of thinking: analytical, sequential, interpersonal, and imaginative. Each individual tends to favor one type of thinking over another, and this thinking preference evolves continually throughout a person's life. In fact, the brain changes all the time with new input and new ways of thinking—a feature that is known as *plasticity*.

Although each person has a preferred thinking style, he or she may prefer it to varying degrees. To identify a person's thinking preference, Herrmann developed the Herrmann Brain Dominance Instrument in 1979. Learning about your own thinking and learning preferences can motivate you to learn new ways to learn and think. For trainers and facilitators, learning about your own preferences can help you identify where you may be neglecting other styles or preferences in your training design and delivery. As Ann Herrmann-Nehdi, daughter of Ned Herrmann and researcher in her own right, notes in the *ASTD Handbook for Workplace Learning Professionals*, "Effective learning is whole brained—designing, delivering, and evaluating the learning to best meet the varying needs of diverse learners" (2008, p. 215).

Herrmann-Nehdi continues, "Our knowledge of the brain and its inherent uniqueness shows that each individual is a unique learner with learning experiences, preferences, and avoidances that will be different from those of other learners. This means that learning designs must somehow factor in the uniqueness of the individual learner" (2008, p. 221). That is to say that effective facilitation must provide a blend of learning activities that addresses various thinking processes from analytical to sequential to interpersonal to imaginative. Because each individual has a unique combination of varying preferences for different types of learning, such a blend can engage most learners even when they are not directly learning in their preferred style. Engaging varied thinking styles ensures *whole brain learning*, rather than a narrow focus on one or two thinking styles.

Here are some tips for incorporating whole brain learning into your facilitation:

- Identify your own thinking preferences to avoid getting too one-sided in your presentation. Deliberately include styles you don't typically prefer.

- Recognize that your learners have unique brains that have continually changed as a result of a lifetime of experiences, learning, and ways of thinking.

- Address those variations in learning and thinking preferences by learning different ways to deliver learning, including facts, case studies, metaphors, brainstorming, simulations, quizzes, outlines, procedures, group learning, role plays, and so on to engage their whole brains.

- Avoid diminishing learners' motivation to learn.

- Avoid overwhelming the brain or causing stress. Stick to need-to-know rather than nice-to-know.

Theory Into Practice

These theories (and more that are not addressed here) affect the way the content of the workshop is put together. Some examples of training features that derive from these theories include handouts, research references, and presentation media to read; quiet time to write notes and reflect; opportunities for listening and talking; and exercises for practicing skills. The workshop activities and materials for the programs in this book have taken these theories to heart in their design, providing content, activities, and tools that will appeal to and engage many learning and thinking styles. Additional ways to translate learning and design theory into practice include the following:

Establishing a Framework

For learners to understand the goals of training and how material relates to real work situations, a framework can be helpful. When presenting the training in the context of a framework, trainers should provide an overview of why the organization has decided to undertake the training and why it is important. This explanation should also highlight what the trainer hopes to accomplish and how the skills learned in this training will be useful back on the job.

Objectives and goals of the programs and learning activities are described in this workbook; share those objectives with the learners when discussing the purposes of specific exercises. Handouts will also help provide a framework for participants.

Identifying Behaviors

Within any training goal are many behaviors. For example, listening and giving clear directions are necessary behaviors for good customer service. Customer service does not improve simply because employees are told to do so—participants need to understand the reasons and see the relevant parts of the equation. For these reasons, facilitators should identify and discuss relevant behaviors throughout the program.

Training helps people identify the behaviors that are important, so that those behaviors can be targeted for improvement. Learning activities enable participants to analyze different skills and behaviors and to separate the parts from the whole. The learning activities in this book, with their clearly stated objectives, have been carefully crafted to take these considerations into account.

Practicing

Practice is crucial for learning because learning takes place by doing and by seeing. In the training designs included in this workbook, practice occurs in written exercises, verbal exercises, and role playing. Role playing helps participants actually practice the behaviors that are being addressed. Role-play exercises bring skills and behaviors to life for those acting out particular roles and for those observing the scenarios.

Learning a new skill takes a lot of practice. Some participants learn skills more quickly than others. Some people's attitudes might prevent them from being open to trying new behaviors. Your job is to facilitate the session to the best of your ability, taking different learning styles into account. The rest is up to the participants.

Providing Feedback

A key aspect of training is the feedback trainers give to participants. If delivered in a supportive and constructive manner, feedback helps learners develop a deeper understanding of the content you are presenting and the behaviors they are practicing. Feedback in role plays is especially powerful because this is where "the rubber hits the road." In role plays, observers can see if people are able to practice the behaviors that have been discussed, or whether habitual responses will prevail.

Making It Relevant

Throughout the program you will discuss how to use skills and new behaviors on the job. These discussions will help answer the question "So what?" Exercises and action plans help participants bring new skills back to actual work situations. This is also important in addressing the adult need for relevancy in learning.

The Bare Minimum

- **Keep the focus on self-reflection.** Be purposeful in designing content that encourages participants to analyze their own behaviors instead of what others do wrong.

- **Build practice into the design.** As with many skills, communication improves with practice. Provide your participants with hands-on, engaging opportunities to practice the correct skills.

Key Points

- Adults have specific learning needs that must be addressed in training to make it successful.

- People also have different intelligences; that is, different areas in which they are more comfortable and competent. Addressing different intelligences in the workshop keeps more people engaged in more ways.

- People take in new information in different ways; so addressing a variety of different thinking styles can help everyone learn more effectively.

- Some important ways of bringing theory into practice are creating a framework, identifying behaviors, practicing, providing feedback, and making the learning relevant.

What to Do Next

- Look through the training materials to identify how they address the learning theories presented in this book. If you make modifications to the material, consider whether those modifications leave out an intelligence or a thinking style. Can you address more intelligences without making the material cumbersome?

- Read the next chapter to identify how to incorporate technology into the workshop to make it more effective.

Additional Resources

Biech, E., ed. (2008). *ASTD Handbook for Workplace Learning Professionals.* Alexandria, VA: ASTD Press.

Biech, E., ed. (2014). *ASTD Handbook: The Definitive Reference for Training & Development,* 2nd edition. Alexandria, VA: ASTD Press.

Gardner, H. (2006). *Multiple Intelligences: New Horizons in Theory and Practice.* New York: Basic Books.

Gardner, H. (2011). *Frames of Mind: The Theory of Multiple Intelligences.* New York: Basic Books.

Herrmann, N. (1988). *Creative Brain.* Lake Lure, NC: Brain Books.

Herrmann, N. (1996). *Whole Brain Business Book.* San Francisco: McGraw-Hill.

Herrmann-Nehdi, A. (2008). "The Learner: What We Need to Know." In E. Biech, ed., *ASTD Handbook for Workplace Learning Professionals,* 2nd edition. Alexandria, VA: ASTD Press.

Jones, J.E., W.L. Bearley, and D.C. Watsabaugh. (1996). *The New Fieldbook for Trainers: Tips, Tools, and Techniques.* Amherst, MA: HRD Press.

Knowles, M.S. (1984). *The Adult Learner: A Neglected Species.* Houston, TX: Gulf Publishing.

Russell, L. (1999). *The Accelerated Learning Fieldbook: Making the Instructional Process Fast, Flexible, and Fun.* San Francisco: Jossey-Bass/Pfeiffer.

Chapter 7

Leveraging Technology to Maximize and Support Design and Delivery

What's in This Chapter

- Recognizing the importance of technology tools
- Determining when to use learning technologies
- Identifying types of learning technologies
- Enhancing learner engagement
- Deepening learner understanding
- Increasing learning application

The workshops offered in this book are designed to be facilitated in person. Even so, learning technologies can and should play a role in adapting workshops to fit your organization, reinforce learning, and measure effectiveness. Technology is an important learning component, but it can also become an expensive distraction. The key is whether and how well technology enhances learners' abilities to understand and apply workshop concepts.

Your use of technology should also align with your organization's culture and readiness. For example, using webinars and wikis in a high-tech environment where employees are familiar with these tools may be logical and welcome, but you might need to introduce these tools more slowly at another company where email is the primary technology used for communication (see Figure 7-1 for some dos and don'ts of recording webinars).

The most important factor to consider when deciding whether to use learning technologies is how they can best support your workshop's learning objectives. This is particularly critical (and not at all straightforward) when delivering this workshop's soft skills training because personal and interpersonal habits and skills tend to require participants to challenge their beliefs and shift their mindsets. This deeper level of self-reflection, though tougher to do in a virtual setting, can be done if you select the right tool and use it at the right time in the learning process.

In the previous chapter, you learned about the adult learning theories and learning styles that underpin the workshops in this volume. Keep these in mind as you assess and weigh opportunities to use learning technologies. In this chapter, you will explore where technology can augment learning transfer and application in your workshop. Please note that the information has been kept general for two reasons. First, each organization has access to specific and limited technologies, and you should learn about them and creatively use what you have. Second, recommendations for specific technologies are likely to become obsolete quickly; so instead, let's focus on the types of learning technologies that might best augment in-person workshops.

Figure 7-1. Dos and Don'ts of Recording Webinars

To increase your chances of a successful webinar, consider and incorporate these tips.

Do
- Introduce yourself and the topic.
- Keep recorded webinars short—ideally 20 minutes or less.
- Use a conversational voice to increase interest.
- Use adequate numbers of slides so that you do not stay on one slide for more than 30 or 45 seconds.
- Address simple, focused topics with five or fewer key points.
- Use pictures and minimal text on slides.

Don't
- Use your computer's microphone to record; instead, invest in a good headset.
- Use a recorded webinar that has poor audio quality; instead, re-record if needed.
- Use too much text or small fonts.
- Assume that participants are just watching the webinar; you have to keep their interest or they will get distracted.
- Try to cover a complex topic using a recorded webinar; the webinar should be focused on one topic with a few main points.

Why Consider Learning Technologies?

You have decided to provide in-person workshops and will use the agendas offered in this book to plan and conduct the training. Learning technologies can be essential tools in your tool kit. Most learning does not occur in the classroom. The workshop is important, but it must be supported by strong pre- and post-course reinforcement. To learn something, learners need many points of contact with the new skills and concepts, such as presentation, reflection, discussion, practice, feedback, and exploration. Moreover, most of your participants are very busy and unable to attend multiple in-person pre- or post-course sessions. So to ensure learning transfer, you can augment in-person activities with technology-based engagement. The good news is that you can use technology in many ways to enhance learning, even of soft skills.

Opportunities to Use Learning Technologies

Whether you have many or few technology resources upon which to draw for learning, start by asking yourself this question: For this topic or series, how can I best use technology to increase learner engagement, understanding, and application? You will use these criteria to discover and evaluate potential ways technology might provide value in the learning process, including

- when designing the training
- before the training

A Note from the Author: Using Technology for Coaching Skills Training

The best coaching training emphasizes practice, and so any technology you use will need to enable discussion. Participants can practice over the telephone, through online web meetings, and with video conferencing. It is not advisable, however, to cut out the one-on-one practicing to add more content. You can also use a combination of delivery methods. For example, I have led webinars to present the content and then broke the group into discussion pairs who would call each other (pairings and contact information were shared by email) to do the practice session. Participants then rejoined the webinar after the practice session.

As you have discovered looking over the workshop materials, the Coaching Model shared here does not offer linear steps. Your participants will be given a new mindset to consider and use. You may want to jumpstart the paradigm shift early and share blog posts or online video clips as pre-work.

- during the training
- after the training
- while building a learner community.

Note that this chapter offers ways to use technology to enhance traditional learning workshops (blended learning). We assume you will be consulting with a technology partner if you are considering a technology-driven training program—such as a workplace simulation or self-directed online learning. That said, the content found in this training series could be adapted for use in an online learning platform. For more information on how to use the online tools and downloads, see Chapter 15.

Designing Training

The ATD Workshop Series offers fully designed training you can use with minimal preparation and solid facilitation skills. Even so, you will be creating a learning implementation plan that is an important part of the design process.

To increase engagement: You have to know your audience members to engage them, because engagement is a choice driven by interest, challenge, and relevance of the topic. Use learning technologies to ensure that you understand where your audience is coming from and the learning approaches they will most value. Email groups, online surveys, teleconferencing, and web meetings with polling can help you ascertain their wants and needs before you solidify your training plan.

To deepen understanding: When in the planning stage, make sure that you have not tried to cram too much presentation into the learning process and that you have planned sufficient time and attention to engaging participants. Flowcharting or mind-mapping software can help you visualize and communicate your learning plan and ensure that you allow for maximum engagement and practice.

To increase application: Increasing retention and application requires buy-in from sponsors and managers to ensure that what is learned is welcomed and applied on the job. Use email groups, online surveys, teleconferencing, and web meetings with polling to communicate with sponsors and managers about what they want out of the training and to identify ways to apply the learning back on the job. Having this information is also valuable in developing the training plan.

Before Training

You want to prime your participants' minds for the topic you will be presenting during the workshop. Pre-work does not have to be something arduous and unwelcome. In fact, a great pre-work assignment can help maximize precious time in the classroom and allow you to focus on the topics that require thorough discussion.

To increase engagement: Tap into the most fascinating aspects of the workshop topic and introduce these through video clips, blog posts, and online resources (see Figure 7-2 about the legal use of video clips, images, and so forth). Avoid boring participants with long "how-to" articles or book chapters before the workshop. In fact, do the opposite and ensure that the pre-work is interesting, provocative (even controversial), and brief. You might select a blog post or video clip that offers a counterpoint to the training or something that inspires your participants to think about the topic before attending training.

To deepen understanding: If you know that the workshop topic will be challenging to some of your participants, prepare and share a brief recorded webinar, video clip, or article that introduces the topic. For example, if your managers tend to tell versus coach, try sharing one or two external resources that discuss the value of service-oriented coaching conversations.

Figure 7-2. Copyright Beware

Copyright law is a sticky, complex area that is beyond the scope of this book to address in detail. For legal advice, consult your legal department.

However, it's very important to note a few things about copyright, fair use, and intellectual property:

- Just because you found an image, article, music, or video online doesn't mean that you can use it in training without permission. Make sure you obtain permission from the copyright owner before you use it (sometimes the copyright owner is not obvious and you will need to do some research).

- Fair use is pretty limited. Although most fair use allows an educational exception, that does *not* include corporate or organizational training. Other exceptions relate to how much material relative to the original was used, the nature of the original work (creative work generally has more protection), and the effect on the market for the original (Swindling and Partridge 2008). Once again, your best bet is to get written permission.

- Just because something doesn't have a copyright notice on it doesn't mean that it isn't copyright protected. All original material is protected under copyright law as soon as it is published or created.

Don't despair. Plenty of online sources of images, videos, text, and so forth exist that you can use for free or for a minimal fee. Just search on the terms "copyright free" or "open source." Another place to look is Wikimedia Commons, which has millions of freely usable media files. For more information about how copyright law affects your use of materials in this volume, please see Chapter 15 on how to use the online materials and downloads.

To increase application: You can improve the chances that your participants will apply what they learn by ensuring they identify real-world work challenges in which they can apply their new skills. Start with a one- or two-question pre-workshop survey (using Survey Monkey or similar) that requires they identify these opportunities and then use the responses to enhance your in-workshop discussions. If your organization has an internal social network or ways to create collaboration groups, use the pre-work questions to begin an online discussion of the topic. The conversations will help your participants think about the topic and will help you prepare for a great workshop (and will give you a beneficial "heads-up" on potential areas of conflict or disagreement).

During Training

Learning technologies can help make your workshops more interesting and can help enhance understanding of the material. Beware, however, that you always want to have a "Plan B" in case of technology glitches or breakdowns. Another critical point to make here is that technology does not change how people learn. Learning and performance drive the technology choice, not the other way around.

To increase engagement: The perennial favorite technology for spicing up a workshop is the use of a great video. Boring videos don't help! If you can find short video clips that reinforce your most important points, please do so. In addition to adding contrast to the workshop flow, having other "experts" say what you want participants to hear is helpful. Another way to increase engagement is to use some kind of audience-response system or electronic polling. Although this might not be practical for small groups (the technology can be a bit pricey), some less expensive alternatives use texting schemas you might want to check out. Your participants will love seeing their collective responses instantly populate your PowerPoint charts. (For more on PowerPoint, see Figure 7-3 and Chapter 8.)

To deepen understanding: Videos can also help improve understanding. If your participants have access to computers during the workshop, consider short technology-based games and short simulations that reinforce the points. You can also ask participants to fill out worksheets and surveys online during the class. Share animated models, flowcharts, or mind maps to help explain key concepts or how they connect together.

To increase application: Learning simulations and practice sessions help prepare participants to apply new skills. You can do these in person, and you can use technology to facilitate practices. This depends a lot on the topic.

After Training

Your participants are busy, and the new skills and concepts they learned in the workshop will become a distant memory without follow-up. Just as you did before the training, you can and should use learning technologies to augment the learning that occurs during the workshop.

To increase engagement: Learners engage when they perceive something as interesting, relevant right now, or challenging. Use tools such as video, blogs, social networks, chat, websites, and email to increase interest in the topic and to provide challenge.

To deepen understanding: Use post-workshop surveys and polling tools to assess understanding so you can address any gap. Add to the participants' understanding of the topic by posting materials on a SharePoint site or through blog posts that you push to their email inboxes using an RSS feed.

To increase application: Provide a just-in-time online resource where participants find quick reference sheets and get application tips using a group site, social network, or SharePoint site. Request or require that participants report how they have used new skills through an online project management collaboration site, wiki, or email group.

Building a Learning Community

Creating an ongoing network of learners is extremely valuable, especially for soft skills. The in-person workshop is just the beginning of the learning journey and so keeping learners engaged is helpful. In addition, you want to create a safe place where learners can discuss challenges, provide encouragement, and share their best practices. Learning technologies are particularly useful for building community among learners and teams.

Figure 7-3. PowerPoint or Prezi or Other?

Although PowerPoint is the most common presentation software, other platforms you might want to consider include Prezi, GoAnimate, Google Docs, mind-mapping programs, or others. Here are a few key considerations that will help you choose:

- Aside from the in-class workshop, where will you want to share the presentation?
- If you will be sharing the presentation with others, consider whether new software will be required.
- Which presentation platform is best for the content you are presenting, or does it matter?
- What are the costs and resources required for each platform?
- Which platform will partner well with technology tools you will use to reinforce the learning?
- What might be the advantage of using two or more platforms throughout the learning process?

To increase engagement: Busy people value community but often can't make the time to attend follow-up sessions or network with peers. They might, however, be able to take 10 minutes to check in on an internal social network, group site, or blog to learn from and share with others. If your organization does not have social networking or collaboration software, you might need to get creative. Talk to your technology department about the tools you do have—whether they are SharePoint, blog software, internal messaging, a wiki-type project management collaboration tool, or other. You can even use email groups to connect learners. Look for ways you can create pull (they choose when to engage) and push (they get updates), such as using RSS feeds.

To deepen understanding: After the workshop, use web meetings, teleconferencing, and messaging to connect learning partners or mentors and facilitate their sharing real-time application stories. Periodically facilitate online discussion groups to reinforce the learning and bring participants back together.

To increase application: Use a collaborative online project site or social network to set expectations about post-workshop peer discussions and reinforce engagement. Poll participants and assign sub-teams to lead a portion of each web meeting.

The Bare Minimum

- **Know what resources you have available.** Many organizations have widely varying resources; don't assume that you know everything that is available.

- **Stretch yourself.** Be willing to try something new; develop your skills to use technology, in innovative ways to facilitate learning.

- **Know your participants.** They may be far ahead of you in their skills with technology or they may be far behind. If you plan to use learning technologies, do your best to assess their skill level before designing the workshop.

- **Be prepared for challenges.** It seems that no matter the skill level of the group, technology glitches are unavoidable. Be sure to cultivate good working relationships with technology support staff.

Key Points

- Most learning does not happen in a classroom but through multiple points of reinforcement. Learning technologies are an efficient way to augment learning.

- You can use learning technologies your organization already has if you are creative and partner with your technology team.

- Use learning technologies throughout the learning process to increase engagement, understanding, and application.

What to Do Next

- **Highlight the portions of this chapter that seem most relevant to your learning plan.** Meet with your technology team and get its input on the most applicable tools you might use.

- **Create a plan for how you will use learning technologies to reinforce your workshop.** Ensure that you select only those tools and activities that will enhance the overall learning objectives and be mindful of your organization's culture and comfort level with technology.

- **Test, test, test!** Practice using technology tools to ensure they will deliver what you hope.

- **Read the next chapter to learn ways you can improve your facilitation skills.** Many of these skills will also be useful when using learning technologies, especially collaboration tools.

Additional Resources

Bozarth, J. (2014). "Effective Social Media for Learning." In E. Biech, ed., *ASTD Handbook: The Definitive Reference for Training & Development,* 2nd edition. Alexandria, VA: ASTD Press.

Chen, J. (2012). *50 Digital Team-Building Games: Fast, Fun Meeting Openers, Group Activities and Adventures Using Social Media, Smart Phones, GPS, Tablets, and More.* Hoboken, NJ: Wiley.

Halls, J. (2012). *Rapid Video Development for Trainers: How to Create Learning Videos Fast and Affordably.* Alexandria, VA: ASTD Press.

Kapp, K. (2013). *The Gamification of Learning and Instruction Fieldbook: Ideas into Practice.* San Francisco: Wiley.

Palloff, R.M., and K. Pratt. (2009). *Building Online Learning Communities: Effective Strategies for the Virtual Classroom.* San Francisco: Jossey-Bass.

Quinn, C. (2014). "M-Thinking: There's an App for That." In E. Biech, ed., *ASTD Handbook: The Definitive Reference for Training & Development,* 2nd edition. Alexandria, VA: ASTD Press.

Swindling, L.B., and M.V.B. Partridge. (2008). "Intellectual Property: Protect What Is Yours and Avoid Taking What Belongs to Someone Else." In E. Biech, *ASTD Handbook for Workplace Learning Professionals.* Alexandria, VA: ASTD Press.

Toth, T. (2006). *Technology for Trainers.* Alexandria, VA: ASTD Press.

Udell, C. (2012). *Learning Everywhere: How Mobile Content Strategies Are Transforming Training.* Nashville, TN: Rockbench Publishing.

Chapter 8

Delivering Your Coaching Workshop: Be a Great Facilitator

What's in This Chapter

- Defining the facilitator's role
- Creating an effective learning environment
- Preparing participant materials
- Using program preparation checklists
- Starting and ending on a strong note
- Managing participant behaviors

Let's get one thing clear from the get-go: Facilitating a workshop—facilitating learning—is *not* lecturing. The title of ATD's bestselling book says it all: *Telling Ain't Training* (Stolovitch and Keeps 2011). A facilitator is the person who helps learners open themselves to new learning and makes the process easier. The role requires that you avoid projecting yourself as a subject matter expert (SME) and that you prepare activities that foster learning through "hands-on" experience and interaction.

Before you can help someone else learn, you must understand the roles you will embody when you deliver training: trainer, facilitator, and learner. When a workshop begins, you are the trainer, bringing to the learning event a plan, structure, experience, and objectives. This is only possible because you have a strong, repeatable logistics process. As you ask the learners to prioritize the learning objectives, you slowly release control, inviting them to become partners in their own learning. As you move from the trainer role into the facilitator role, the objectives are the contract between the learners and the facilitator. All great facilitators also have a third role in the classroom—the role of learner. If you are open, you can learn many new things when you are in class. If you believe you must be the expert as a learning facilitator, you will not be very effective.

To be most successful as a learning facilitator, consider this checklist:

- ☐ Identify the beliefs that limit your ability to learn and, therefore, to teach.
- ☐ Learning is a gift for you and from you to others.
- ☐ Choose carefully what you call yourself and what you call your outcomes.
- ☐ Clarify your purpose to better honor your roles at a learning event.
- ☐ If you can't teach with passion, don't do it.

This last point is especially important. Not everyone is destined to be a great facilitator and teacher, but you can still have enormous impact if you are passionate about the topic, the process, and about helping people improve their working lives. If you are serious about becoming a great facilitator, Chapter 13 provides a comprehensive assessment instrument to help you manage your personal development and increase the effectiveness of your training (see Assessment 3). You can use this instrument for self-assessment, end-of-course feedback, observer feedback, or as a professional growth tracker.

With these points firmly in mind—facilitating is not lecturing and passion can get you past many facilitator deficiencies—let's look at some other important aspects of facilitating, starting with how to create an engaging and effective learning environment.

The Learning Environment

Colors, seating, tools, environmental considerations (such as temperature, ventilation, lighting), and your attitude, dress, preparation, and passion all enhance—or detract from—an effective and positive learning environment. This section describes some ways to maximize learning through environmental factors.

Color. Research has shown that bland, neutral environments are so unlike the real world that learning achieved in these "sensory deprivation chambers" cannot be transferred to the job.

Color can be a powerful way to engage the limbic part of the brain and create long-term retention. It can align the right and left brains. Ways to incorporate color include artwork, plants, and pictures that help people feel comfortable and visually stimulated. Consider printing your handouts and assessments in color. The training support materials provided in this book are designed in color but can be printed either color or in grayscale (to reduce reproduction costs).

Room Setup. Because much learning requires both individual reflection and role playing, consider seating that promotes personal thought and group sharing. One way to accomplish this is to set up groups of three to five at round or square tables, with each chair positioned so the projection screen can easily be seen. Leave plenty of room for each person so that when he or she does need to reflect, there is a feeling of privacy. Keep in mind that comfortable chairs and places to write help people relax to learn. Figure 8-1 details more room configurations that you can use to accomplish specific tasks or purposes in training.

Tools of the Trade. Lots of flipcharts (one per table is optimal) with brightly colored markers create an interactive environment. Flipcharts are about as basic and low tech as tools get, but they are also low cost and do the trick. Consider putting colorful hard candy on the tables (include sugar-free options), with bright cups of markers, pencils, and pens. Gather pads of colorful sticky notes and "fidgets" (quiet toys such as chenille stems, koosh balls, and others) to place on the table as well. For the right level of trust to exist, your learners must feel welcome.

Your Secret Weapon. Finally, the key to establishing the optimal learning environment is *you*. You set the tone by your attitude, the way you greet people, the clothes you wear, your passion, and your interest and care for the participants. You set the stage for learning with four conditions that only you as the facilitator can create to maximize learning:

1. **Confidentiality.** Establish the expectation that anything shared during the training program will remain confidential among participants and that as the facilitator you are committed to creating a safe environment. An important step in learning is first admitting ignorance, which has some inherent risk. Adult learners may resist admitting their learning needs because they fear the repercussions of showing their weaknesses. You can alleviate these concerns by assuring participants that the sole purpose of the training is to build their skills, and that no evaluations will take place. Your workshop must be a safe place to learn and take risks.

Figure 8-1. Seating Configurations

Select a room setup that will best support the needs of your learners:

- **Rounds.** Circular tables are particularly useful for small-group work when you have 16 to 24 participants.

- **U-Shaped.** This setup features three long rectangular tables set up to form a U, with you at the open end. It is good for overall group interaction and small-group work (two to three people). This setup also helps you establish rapport with your learners.

- **Classroom.** This setup is a traditional grade school format characterized by rows of tables with all the participants facing forward toward the trainer. Avoid this setup as much as possible because you become the focal point rather than the learners, and your ability to interact with learners is extremely limited. Problems of visibility also occur when rows in the back are blocked by rows in the front.

- **Chevron.** Chevron setup features rows of tables as in the classroom setup but the tables are angled to form a V-shape. This opens up the room to allow you to interact more with the learners and accommodates a larger group of learners without sacrificing visibility. However, it shares many of the drawbacks of the classroom setup.

- **Hybrid or Fishbone.** This setup combines a U-shaped configuration with that of a chevron. It is useful when there are too many learners to form a good U and there is room enough to broaden the U to allow tables to be set up as chevrons in the center of the U. This hybrid approach allows for interaction and enables the trainer to move around.

Source: Drawn from D.V. McCain and D.D. Tobey. (2004). *Facilitation Basics*. Alexandria, VA: ASTD Press.

2. **Freedom from distractions.** Work and personal demands cannot be ignored during training, but to maximize each participant's learning, and as a courtesy to others, outside demands should be minimized.

   a. Select a training site away from the workplace to help reduce distractions.

   b. Acknowledge that participants probably feel they shouldn't be away from work; remind them that the purpose of the training is to improve their work lives.

   c. Ask that cell phones and pagers be turned off or set to silent alerts.

   d. Emphasize that because they are spending this time in training, trainees should immerse themselves in the learning experience and thereby maximize the value of their time away from work responsibilities.

3. **Personal responsibility for learning.** A facilitator can only create the *opportunity* for learning. Experiential learning requires that participants actively engage with and commit to learning—they cannot sit back and soak up information like sponges.

4. **Group participation.** Each participant brings relevant knowledge to the training program. Through discussion and sharing of information, a successful training session will tap into the knowledge of each participant. Encourage all participants to accept responsibility for helping others learn.

Program Preparation Checklist

Preparation is power when it comes to facilitating a successful workshop, and a checklist is a powerful tool for effective preparation. This checklist of activities will help you prepare your workshop:

☐ Write down all location and workshop details when scheduling the workshop.

☐ Make travel reservations early (to save money, too), if applicable.

☐ Send a contract to the client to confirm details, or if you are an internal facilitator, develop guidelines and a workshop structure in conjunction with appropriate supervisors and managers.

☐ Specify room and equipment details in writing and then confirm by telephone.

☐ Define goals and expectations for the workshop.

☐ Get a list of participants, titles, roles, and responsibilities.

☐ Send participants a questionnaire that requires them to confirm their goals for the workshop.

☐ Send the client (or the participants, if you are an internal facilitator) an agenda for the workshop, with times for breaks and meals.

☐ Recommend that lunch or dinner be offered in-house, with nutritious food provided.

☐ Make a list of materials that you will need in the room (pads of paper, pens, pencils, markers, flipcharts, and so forth). Make sure to plan for some extras.

☐ Design the room layout (for example, U-shaped, teaching style, auditorium setup, or half-circle).

☐ Confirm whether you or your internal/external client will prepare copies of the workshop handouts. The workshop handouts should include all tools, training instruments, assessments, and worksheets. You may choose also to include copies of the PowerPoint slides as part of the participant guide. All the supplemental materials you need to conduct the workshops in this book are available for download (see Chapter 15 for instructions).

☐ Find out if participants would like to receive pre-reading materials electronically before the session.

☐ Prepare assessments, tools, training instruments, and workshop materials at least one week before the workshop so that you have time to peruse and check them and assemble any equipment you may need (see the next two sections).

Participant Materials

Participant materials support participant learning throughout the workshop and provide continuing references after the workshop has ended. There are several kinds of participant materials. Here are some options:

Handouts

The development and "look" of your handouts are vital to help participants understand the information they convey. To compile the handouts properly, first gather all assessments, tools, training instruments, activities, and PowerPoint slides and arrange them in the order they appear in the workshop. Then bind them together in some fashion. There are several options for compiling your material, ranging from inexpensive to deluxe. The kind of binding is your choice—materials can be stapled, spiral bound, or gathered in a ring binder—but remember that a professional look supports success. Your choice of binding will depend on your budget for the project. Because first appearances count, provide a cover with eye-catching colors and appropriate graphics.

Using the agendas in Chapters 1–3, select the presentation slides, learning activities, handouts, tools, and assessments appropriate to your workshop (see Chapter 15: Online Tools and Downloads). If you choose to print out the presentation slides for your participants, consider printing no more than three slides per handout page to keep your content simple with sufficient white space for the participants to write their own notes. Use the learning objectives for each workshop to provide clarity for the participants at the outset. Remember to number the pages, to add graphics for interest (and humor), and to include tabs for easy reference if the packet of materials has multiple sections.

Some participants like to receive the handouts before the workshop begins. You may want to email participants to determine if they would like to receive the handouts electronically.

Presentation Slides

This ATD Workshop Series book includes presentation slides to support the two-day, one-day, and half-day agendas. They have been crafted to adhere to presentation best practices. If you choose to reorder or otherwise modify the slides, keep in mind these important concepts.

When you use PowerPoint software as a teaching tool, be judicious in the number of slides that you prepare. In a scientific lecture, slides are usually a necessity for explaining formulas or results, but a communication workshop relies on interaction so keep the slide information simple. Also, do not include more than five or six bullet points per slide. See more tips for effective PowerPoint slides in Figure 8-2.

A message can be conveyed quickly through the use of simple graphics. For example, an illustration of two people in conversation may highlight interpersonal communication; a photo of a boardroom-style meeting may illustrate a group engaged in negotiation.

When you use presentation slides ask yourself: What will a slide add to my presentation? Ensure that the answer that comes back is "it will enhance the message." If slides are simply used to make the workshop look more sophisticated or technical, the process may not achieve the desired results.

It can be frustrating when a facilitator shows a slide for every page that the participants have in front of them. The dynamics of the class are likely to disconnect. If the information you are teaching is in the handouts or workbook, work from those media alone and keep the workshop personally interactive.

Workbooks and Journals

A participant journal can be included in the binder with your handouts, or it may be a separate entity. Throughout the workshop participants can assess their progress and advance their development by entering details of their personal learning in the journal. The benefit of this journal to participants is that they can separate their personal discoveries and development from the main workshop handouts and use this journal as an action plan if desired.

Videos

If you show a video in your workshop, ensure that the skills it contains are up to date and that the video is less than 20 minutes long. Provide questions that will lead to a discussion of the information viewed. Short video clips can be effective learning tools.

Toys, Noisemakers, and Other Props

Experienced facilitators understand the value of gadgets and games that advance the learning, provide a break from learning, or both.

Adults love to play. When their minds are open they learn quickly and effectively. Something as simple as tossing a rubber ball from person to person as questions are asked about elements studied can liven up the workshop and help people remember what they've learned.

Figure 8-2. Tips for Effective PowerPoint Slides

Presentation slides can enhance your presentation. They can also detract from it by being too cluttered, monotonous, or hard to read. Here are some tips for clear, effective slides:

Fonts

- Use sans-serif fonts such as Arial, Calibri, or Helvetica; other fonts are blurry when viewed from 20 feet or more and are more easily read on LCD screens and in video/web presentations.
- Use the same sans-serif font for most (if not all) of the presentation.
- Use a font size no smaller than 24 points. (This will also help keep the number of bullets per slide down.)
- Consider using a 32-point font—this is the easiest for web/video transmission.
- Limit yourself to one font size per slide.

Colors

- Font colors should be black or dark blue for light backgrounds and white or yellow on dark backgrounds. Think high contrast for clarity and visual impact.
- Avoid using red or green. It doesn't project well, doesn't transfer well when used in a webinar, and causes issues for people who suffer color blindness.

Text and Paragraphs

- Align text left or right, not centered.
- Avoid cluttering a slide—use a single headline and a few bullet points.
- Use no more than six words to a line; avoid long sentences.
- Use sentence case—ALL CAPS ARE DIFFICULT TO READ AND CAN FEEL LIKE YELLING.
- Avoid abbreviations and acronyms.
- Limit use of punctuation marks.

Source: Cat Russo (2014).

Case studies and lively exercises accelerate learning. Bells and whistles are forms of communication; use them when you pit two teams against each other or to indicate the end of an activity.

Facilitator Equipment and Materials

When all details for the workshop have been confirmed, it is time to prepare for the actual facilitation of the workshop at the site. You may know the site well because you are providing in-house facilitation. If, however, you are traveling off site to facilitate, important elements enter the planning. Here's a checklist of things to consider:

☐ Pack a data-storage device that contains your handouts and all relevant workshop materials. In the event that your printed materials do not reach the workshop location, you will have the electronic files to reprint on site.

- [ ] Pack the proper power cords, a spare battery for the laptop, and a bulb for the LCD or overhead projector in the event that these items are not available at the workshop location. This requires obtaining the make and model of all audiovisual and electronic equipment from the client or the training facility during your planning process.

- [ ] Bring an extension cord.

- [ ] Bring reference materials, books, article reprints, and ancillary content. Take advantage of all technology options, such as Kindles or other readers to store reference materials. As a facilitator, you will occasionally need to refer to materials other than your own for additional information. Having the materials with you not only provides correct information about authors and articles, but it also positively reinforces participants' impressions of your knowledge, training, openness to learning, and preparedness.

- [ ] Bring flipcharts, painter's tape, and sticky notes.

- [ ] Pack toys and games for the workshop, a timer or bell, and extra marking pens.

- [ ] Bring duct tape. You may need it to tape extension cords to the floor as a safety precaution. The strength of duct tape also ensures that any flipchart pages hung on walls (with permission) will hold fast. Or, worst-case scenario, the duct tape can be used to contain unruly participants!

You can ship these items to the workshop in advance, but recognize that the shipment may not arrive in time, and that even if it does arrive on time, you may have to track it down at the venue. Also, take some time identifying backups or alternatives in case the materials, technology, and so on do not conform to plan. What are the worst-case scenarios? How could you manage such a situation? Prepare to be flexible and creative.

A Strong Start: Introduction, Icebreakers, and Openers

The start of a session is a crucial time in the workshop dynamic. How the participants respond to you, the facilitator, can set the mood for the remainder of the workshop. To get things off on the right foot, get to the training room early, at least 30 to 60 minutes before the workshop. This gives you time not only to set up the room if that has not already been done, but also to test the environment, the seating plan, the equipment, and your place in the room. Find out where the restrooms are. When participants begin to arrive (and some of them come very early), be ready to welcome them. Don't be distracted with problems or issues; be free and available to them.

While they are settling in, engage them with simple questions:

- How was your commute?
- Have you traveled far for this workshop?

- Was it easy to find this room?
- May I help you with anything?

When the participants have arrived and settled, introduce yourself. Write a humorous introduction, if that's your style, because this will help you be more approachable. Talk more about what you want to accomplish in the workshop than about your accomplishments. If you have a short biographical piece included in the handouts or in the workbook, it may serve as your personal introduction.

At the conclusion of your introduction, provide an activity in which participants can meet each other (often called an icebreaker). Because participants sometimes come into a training session feeling inexperienced, skeptical, reluctant, or scared, using icebreaker activities to open training enables participants to interact in a fun and nonthreatening way and to warm up the group before approaching more serious content. Don't limit the time on this too much unless you have an extremely tight schedule. The more time participants spend getting to know each other at the beginning of the workshop, the more all of you will benefit as the session proceeds.

Feedback

Feedback is the quickest, surest way for you, the facilitator, to learn if the messages and instruction are reaching the participants and if the participants are absorbing the content. It is also important for you to evaluate the participants' rate of progress and learning. Answers to the questions you ask throughout the workshop will help you identify much of the progress, but these answers come from only a few of the participants at a time. They're not a global snapshot of the entire group's comprehension and skills mastery.

When you lead a workshop, the participants walk a fine line between retention and deflection of knowledge. Continuing evaluations ensure that learning is taking root. Three levels of questions—learning comprehension, skills mastery, and skills application—help you determine where the training may not be achieving the intended results.

- Learning comprehension checks that the participants understand and grasp the skills being taught (see Figure 8-3).
- Skills mastery means that the participants are able to demonstrate their newly acquired knowledge by some activity, such as teaching a portion of a module to their fellow participants or delivering their interpretation of topic specifics to the class (see Figure 8-4).
- Skills application is the real test. You may choose to substantiate this through role plays or group case studies. When the participants have the opportunity to verbally communicate

the skills learned and to reach desired results through such application, then skills application is established (see Figure 8-5).

The questions in Figures 8-3 to 8-5 are designed for written answers so you can incorporate them into the takeaway workbook you create. The questions concerning skills mastery and skills application could be set as homework if the workshop is longer than one day. Keep in mind that you will also reevaluate after each day of a multiday session.

Let's now look at other forms of in-class learning assessments: role plays, participant presentations, ball toss, and journaling.

Role Plays

Role plays are an effective tool for assessing learning comprehension. If two or more participants conduct a role play that reveals their understanding of the information, with an outcome that reflects that understanding, then it becomes a "live feed," instantaneous learning for all.

You must set up the role play carefully. It is often wise for you to be a part of the first role-play experience to show participants how it's done and to make them more comfortable with the activity. Ensure that you explain all the steps of the role play and the desired outcome. It is insightful to role-play a negative version first, followed by participant discussion; then role-play a positive aspect the second time. For example, if confrontational communication is the topic and the situation under discussion involves a line manager and his or her supervisor, first enact the role play using the verbal and body language that is causing the negative result. Discuss this as a class to identify the specific language that needs improvement. Then enact the role play again, this time using positive language.

Frequently it is helpful for a participant who has been on the receiving end of negative communication in his or her workplace to adopt the role of deliverer. Walking in the other person's

Figure 8-3. Learning Comprehension Questions

Here are some questions that can be asked to determine each participant's level of *learning comprehension*:

- Give a brief overview of your learning in this workshop. (Begin your phrases with "I have learned. . . ." This will assist you in focusing your responses.)
- How/where will you apply this knowledge in your workplace?
- Did you acquire this knowledge through lectures/practice/discussion or a combination of all methods?
- Do you feel sufficiently confident to pass on this knowledge to your colleagues?
- Are there any areas that will require additional learning for you to feel sufficiently confident?

Figure 8-4. Skills Mastery Questions

Now let's look at some questions you can use to evaluate your trainees' *skills mastery*:

- If you were asked to teach one skill in this workshop, which skill would it be?
- What would your three key message points be for that skill?
- Describe the steps you would take to instruct each message point (for example, lecture, group discussion, PowerPoint presentation, and so forth).
- What methods would you use to ensure that your participants comprehend your instruction?
- Would feedback from your participants, both positive and negative, affect the development of your skills mastery? If yes, illustrate your response and the changes you would make.

Figure 8-5. Skills Application Questions

And finally, let's consider some questions that identify participants' *ability to apply the skills* they've learned in the workshop:

- Please describe a situation at your workplace where you could employ one specific communication skill from this workshop.
- How would you introduce this skill to your colleagues?
- How would you set goals to measure the improvement in this skill?
- Describe the input and participation you would expect from your colleagues.
- How would you exemplify mastery of the skill?

shoes leads to a quicker understanding of the transaction. This positive role play should also be followed by whole-group discussion of the elements that worked. Participants can be invited to write about the process and its results to give them a real-life example to take back to the workplace.

Participant Presentations

You might ask a participant to present a module of learning to the workshop. This allows the facilitator to observe the participants from a different perspective—both as listeners and as presenters. Be ready to assist or to answer questions. For example, a participant may choose assertive communication as his or her module, and the specific issue on return to the workplace may be a request for promotion. The participant defines and delivers the steps required to ask for the promotion while the facilitator and other participants observe and evaluate the success of the approach and demonstration of confidence and assertiveness.

Ball Toss

A quick method for evaluating a class's knowledge of the material presented is to ask the participants to form a standing circle. The facilitator throws out a soft rubber ball to an individual and asks a question about the previous learning activity. When the catcher gives the right answer, he or she throws the ball to another participant who answers another question. The facilitator can step out of this circle and let the participants ask as well as answer questions to review the skills as a group. Candy for all as a reward for contributions is always enjoyed by the participants (consider keeping some sugar-free treats on hand as well).

Journaling

Keeping a journal is a quiet, introspective way for participants to get a grip on their learning. When you complete an activity, have everyone take five minutes to write a summary of the skill just learned and then ask them to share what they've written with a partner. Invite the partner to correct and improve the material if necessary or appropriate.

Questioning Skills

When participants are asking questions, they are engaged and interested. Your responses to questions will augment the learning atmosphere. The way in which you respond is extremely important. Answers that are evasive can disturb a class because they cast doubts on your credibility. Glib or curt answers are insulting. Lengthy responses break the rhythm of the class and often go off track. When dealing with questions, the value of effective communication is in hearing the question, answering the question asked, and moving on. Repeat questions so that all participants hear them. In addition, this can ensure that you have heard the question correctly.

However, don't rush to answer. Take time to let everyone absorb the information. When time is of the essence, don't be tempted to give long, complicated answers that embrace additional topics. Be courteous and clear. Check that your answer has been understood. When a question comes up that could possibly derail the session or that is beyond the scope of the topic, you can choose to record it on a "parking lot" list and then revisit it later at an assigned time. A parking lot can be as simple as a list on a flipchart. However, whenever possible, answer a question at the time it is asked. Consider answering with analogies when they are appropriate because these often help elucidate challenging concepts.

Effective questions that prompt answers are open ended:

- What have you learned so far?
- How do you feel about this concept?
- How would you handle this situation?

Any question that begins with "what" or "how" promotes a more extensive answer. Questions that begin with "why"—as in "why do you think that way?"—can promote defensiveness.

When a participant asks a confrontational or negative question, handle it with dignity and do not become aggressive. It's helpful to ask open-ended questions of the participant to try to clarify the original question. For example, ask, "What do you mean by . . . ?" or "Which part of the activity do you find challenging?" This form of open-ended questioning requires additional accountability from the participant. The reason for the confrontation may have arisen from confusion about the information or the need to hear his or her own thoughts aloud. When you are calm and patient, the altercation is more likely to be resolved. If the participant persists, you may wish to ask him or her to discuss the specifics in a private setting. More ideas for dealing with difficult participants are provided later in this chapter.

Some participants enjoy being questioned because it gives them an opportunity to show their knowledge. Others are reticent for fear of looking foolish if they don't know the answer. Because your trainees have unique styles and personalities, always have a purpose for asking questions: Will these questions test the participants' knowledge? Are these questions appropriate? Are you asking them in the style that suits the participant?

Training Room and Participant Management

When everything is in place and ready for the session, it's time to review the "soft skills" portion of your responsibilities—that is, how you conduct the workshop and interact with participants. Here are some things to consider:

- **"Respect and respond" should be a facilitator's mantra.** At all times respect the participants and respond in a timely manner.
- **Learn participants' names at the beginning of the workshop.** Focus on each participant, give a firm handshake, repeat the name in your greeting, and then mentally write the name on the person's forehead. When you have time, survey the room and write down every name without looking at nametags or name tents on the tables.
- **Manage workshop program time.** This is vital because it ensures that the goals will be met in the time allotted.
- **Read the participants' body language.** This will help you know when to pause and ask questions or to give them a stretch break.
- **Answer questions fully and effectively.** If you don't know an answer, open the question up to the participants or offer to get back to the questioner. Make a note to remind yourself to do so.

- **Add a "parking lot" to the room**—a large sheet of paper taped to one of the walls (use your own artistic prowess to draw a vehicle of some sort). When questions arise that are out of step with the current communication activity, ask the participant to write the question on a sticky note and put it in the parking lot. When the current activity is completed, you can address the questions parked there.

- **Control unruly participants through assertiveness of vocal tone and message.** When appropriate, invite them to help you with tasks because frequently they just need to be more physically involved. If the unruliness gets out of hand, accompany the person out of the room to discuss the situation.

- **Be sure to monitor a participant who is slower to assimilate the information.** If time permits, give that trainee some one-on-one time with you.

- **Keep your energy high.** Inject humor wherever possible. Ensure the learning is taking root.

A Word About Dealing With Difficult Participants

Much of the preparation you do before a training session will help you minimize disruptive behavior in your training session. But, sadly, you are still likely at some point to have difficult participants in your training room. Beyond preparation, you may need some specific strategies to help you manage disruptions and keep the learning on track. Figure 8-6, drawn from McCain and Tobey's *Facilitation Basics* (2004), identifies many of these behaviors and gives strategies for nipping them in the bud.

Figure 8-6. Managing Difficult Participants

THE PROBLEM	THE SOLUTION
Carrying on a Side Conversation	• Don't assume the talkers are being disrespectful; depersonalize the behavior by thinking: "Maybe they are unclear about a point in the material, or the material is not relevant to their needs." • Ask the talkers if they don't understand something. • Walk toward the talkers as you continue to make your point; this stops many conversations dead in their tracks.
Monopolizing the Discussion	• Some participants tend to take over the conversation; while the enthusiasm is great, you don't want to leave other learners out. • Tell the monopolizer that her comments are valuable and interesting, but you would like to open up the discussion to others in the group. Then call on another person by name. • Enlist the monopolizer to help you by being a gatekeeper and ensuring that no one monopolizes the conversation.
Complaining	• Don't assume someone who complains doesn't have a valid reason to do so. • Ask the rest of the group if they feel the same way. If they do, try to address the issue as appropriate. • If they don't, talk to the individual in the hallway during the break.
Challenging Your Knowledge	• Determine if this person really knows more than you do, or is just trying to act as though he does. • If he does know more, try to enlist his help in the training. • If he doesn't, ask him to provide expertise and he will usually realize he can't and back down.
Daydreaming	• Use the person's name in an example to get her attention. • Switch to something more active. • If behavior affects more than just one person, try to find out if something work-related is causing it and have a brief discussion about it.
Heckling	• Don't get upset or start volleying remarks. • Try giving the person learning-oriented attention: "John, you clearly have some background in this area; would you care to share your thoughts with the rest of the group?" • Get the attention off you by switching to a group-oriented activity.

THE PROBLEM	THE SOLUTION
Clowning Around	• Give the person attention in a learning-oriented way by calling on her to answer a question or be a team leader. • If a joke is intended to relieve tension in the room and others seem to be experiencing it, deal with the tension head on by bringing it up. • If it is just a joke, and it's funny and appropriate, laugh!
Making an Insensitive Remark	• Remember that if the person truly didn't intend offense, you don't want to humiliate him. But you do need to ensure that the person and everyone else in the room know that you will not tolerate bigoted or otherwise inappropriate remarks. • Give the person a chance to retract what he said by asking if that is what he meant to say. If it wasn't, then move on. • If it was, you need to let the person know that the comment is not in line with the values of your organization and it can't be allowed to continue. • If the person persists, speak to him in the hallway, or as a last resort, ask him to leave.
Doing Other Work	• Talk to the person at a break to find out if the workshop is meeting her needs. • If the person is truly under too much pressure, offer to have her come to another session.
Not Talking	• If you can tell the person is engaged because he is taking notes, maintaining eye contact, or leaning forward, let him alone. • Give the person opportunities to interact at a greater comfort level by participating in small groups or in pairs.
Withdrawing	• Talk to the person at break to find out if something is going on. Deal with the issue as appropriate. • If the person feels excluded, have her act as a team leader for a turn, or ensure that all members of teams are given opportunities to participate.
Missing the Point	• If someone misses the point, be sensitive in dealing with him or her. Try to find something to agree with in his point. • Try to identify what the person is having trouble grasping and clear up the point with an analogy or an example. • Never laugh at the person or otherwise humiliate him.
Playing with Technology	• Minimize distractions by setting specific ground rules for technology use in the training room. (See Chapter 7 for creative ways to use technology to enhance training.) • Direct a training-related question to the person. • If the behavior persists, talk to the person at break to determine if there is an issue with which you can help.

Source: McCain and Tobey (2004).

When all else fails, you have a few last resorts, although you would clearly rather not get to that point. One option is to simply pull aside the individual who is disrupting the class and talk to her privately. Dick Grote suggests in "Dealing with Miscreants, Snivelers, and Adversaries" that you can often catch someone off guard by asking: "Is it personal?" The direct question will usually cause the individual to deny that it is personal. Next, you tell the person that the behavior is unacceptable and that you will speak to a supervisor or training sponsor if it continues. This often works.

However, if it does not work, you can ask to have the person removed or cancel the program and speak to the person's supervisor. Clearly, these are not options to be taken lightly, but realize that they are available when you are faced with truly recalcitrant behavior.

Follow up when you have faced a difficult situation. Take some time to reflect on the event and write down the details of what happened. If possible, get perspectives and feedback from participants who witnessed it. If outside perspectives are not an option, think about the event from the points of view of the disruptive individual and other participants and ask yourself: What went wrong? What went well? How could I manage the situation better next time?

An Unforgettable End

In Biech (2008), contributor Mel Silberman explains that

> [m]any training programs run out of steam in the end. In some cases, participants are marking time until the close is near. In other cases, facilitators are valiantly trying to cover what they haven't got to before time runs out. How unfortunate! What happens at the end needs to be "unforgettable." You want participants to remember what they've learned. You also want participants to think what they've learned has been special. (p. 315)

Silberman suggests considering four areas when preparing to end your workshop:

- How will participants review what you've taught them?
- How will participants assess what they have learned?
- What will participants do about what they have learned?
- How will participants celebrate their accomplishments?

For example, consider what you've learned in this chapter. You've developed a well-rounded picture of what it takes to create an optimal, effective learning environment, from creating an inviting and engaging space to preparing and gathering materials that will make you feel like an organizational champ. You're ready to get the training off to a productive start, to manage difficult participants and situations, and to pull it all together in a powerful way. Now jump down to the end of the chapter to determine what the next steps are and take pride in the preparation that will enable you to adapt and thrive in the training room.

The Bare Minimum

- **Keep things moving.** Create an engaging, interactive environment.

- **Pay attention to the energy in the room.** Be prepared to adjust the activities as needed. Build in content that can be delivered standing or through networking activities to get participants out of their seats when needed.

- **Have fun!** If you create an upbeat tone and enjoy yourself, the participants are likely to have fun as well.

Key Points

- Facilitation is not lecturing. It's providing learning activities and support to make learning easier for the participant.

- Facilitation is not about the facilitator—it's about the learner.

- An inviting space and a safe, collaborative environment are necessary for learning to occur.

- Good facilitation starts with passion and significant attention to preparation.

- A good start sets the tone for the whole training session.

- A strong ending helps learners to remember the training and carry lessons forward into their work.

What to Do Next

- Prepare, modify, and review the training agenda. Use one of the agendas in Section I as a starting point.

- Review the program preparation checklist and work through it step by step.

- Make a list of required participant materials and facilitator equipment and begin assembling them.

- Review all learning activities included in the agenda and start practicing your delivery.

Additional Resources

Biech, E. (2006). *90 World-Class Activities by 90 World-Class Trainers.* San Francisco: John Wiley/Pfeiffer.

Biech, E. (2008). *10 Steps to Successful Training.* Alexandria, VA: ASTD Press.

Biech, E., ed. (2014). *ASTD Handbook: The Definitive Reference for Training & Development.* Alexandria, VA: ASTD Press.

Duarte, N. (2010). *Resonate: Present Visual Stories That Transform Audiences.* Hoboken, NJ: Wiley.

Grote, D. (1998). "Dealing with Miscreants, Snivelers, and Adversaries," *Training & Development*, 52(10), October.

McCain, D.V., and D. Tobey. (2004). *Facilitation Basics.* Alexandria, VA: ASTD Press.

Stolovitch, H.D., and E.J. Keeps. (2011). *Tellling Ain't Training,* 2nd edition. Alexandria, VA: ASTD Press.

Thiagarajan, S. (2005). *Thiagi's Interactive Lectures: Power Up Your Training With Interactive Games and Exercises.* Alexandria, VA: ASTD Press.

Thiagarajan, S. (2006). *Thiagi's 100 Favorite Games.* San Francisco: John Wiley/Pfeiffer.

Chapter 9
Evaluating Workshop Results

What's in This Chapter

- Exploring the reasons to evaluate your program
- Introducing the levels of measurement and what they measure

---

Evaluation represents the last letter of the ADDIE cycle of instructional design (analysis, design, development, implementation, and evaluation). Although evaluation is placed at the end of the model, an argument could be made for including it far earlier, as early as the design and development phase and perhaps even in the analysis phase. Why? Because the goals of the training, or the learning objectives (see Chapter 5), provide insight into what the purpose of the evaluation should be. In fact, business goals, learning goals, and evaluation of those goals are useful subjects to address with organizational leaders or the training sponsor. Trainers often begin a program without thinking about how the program fits into a strategic plan or how it supports and promotes specific business goals, but these are critical to consider before implementing the program.

However, this chapter is not about that upfront evaluation of the program design and materials; it is about evaluating the program after it has been delivered and reporting the results back to the training sponsor. This form of evaluation allows you to determine whether the program objectives were achieved and whether the learning was applied on the job and had an impact on the business. Evaluation can also serve as the basis for future program and budget discussions with training sponsors.

Levels of Measurement

No discussion of measurement would be complete without an introduction to the concepts that underpin the field of evaluation. The following is a brief primer on a very large and detailed subject that can be somewhat overwhelming. If your organization is committed to measuring beyond Level 2, take some time to read the classics of evaluation.

In 1956–57, Donald Kirkpatrick, one of the leading experts in measuring training results, identified four levels of measurement and evaluation. These four levels build successively from the simplest (Level 1) to the most complex (Level 4) levels of evaluation and are based on information gathered at previous levels. For that reason, determining upfront at what level to evaluate a program is important. A general rule of thumb is that the more important or fundamental the training is and the greater the investment in it, the higher the level of evaluation to use. The four basic levels of evaluation are

- **Level 1—Reaction:** Measures how participants react to the workshop.
- **Level 2—Learning:** Measures whether participants have learned and understood the content of the workshop.
- **Level 3—Behavior (also referred to as application):** Measures on-the-job changes that have occurred because of the learning.
- **Level 4—Results:** Measures the impact of training on the bottom line.

These four levels correspond with the evaluation methods described below.

Level 1. Measuring Participant Reactions

One of the most common ways trainers use to measure participants' reactions is by administering end-of-session evaluation forms, often called "smile sheets" (for a sample, see Handout 10: Workshop Evaluation Form). The main benefit of using smile sheets is that they are easy to create and administer. If you choose this method, consider the suggestions below, but first decide the purpose of evaluating. Do you want to know if the participants enjoyed the presentation? How they felt about the facilities? Or how they reacted to the content?

Here are a few suggestions for creating evaluation forms:

- Keep the form to one page.
- Make your questions brief.
- Leave adequate space for comments.

- Group types of questions into categories (for example, cluster questions about content, questions about the instructor, and questions about materials).

- Provide variety in types of questions (include multiple-choice, true-false, short-answer, and open-ended items).

- Include relevant decision makers in your questionnaire design.

- Plan how you will use and analyze the data and create a design that will facilitate your analysis.

- Use positively worded items (such as, "I listen to others," instead of "I don't listen to others").

You can find additional tips for creating smile sheets and evaluating their results in the *Infoline* "Making Smile Sheets Count" by Nancy S. Kristiansen (2004).

Although smile sheets are used frequently, they have some inherent limitations. For example, participants cannot judge the *effectiveness* of training techniques. In addition, results can be overly influenced by the personality of the facilitator or participants' feelings about having to attend training. Be cautious of relying solely on Level 1 evaluations.

Level 2. Measuring the Extent to Which Participants Have Learned

If you want to determine the extent to which participants have understood the content of your workshop, testing is an option. Comparing pre-training and post-training test results indicates the amount of knowledge gained. Or you can give a quiz that tests conceptual information 30 to 60 days after the training to see if people remember the concepts. Because most adult learners do not generally like the idea of tests, you might want to refer to these evaluations as "assessments."

Another model of testing is criterion-referenced testing (CRT), which tests the learner's performance against a given standard, such as "greets the customer and offers assistance within one minute of entering the store" or "initiates the landing gear at the proper time and altitude." Such testing can be important in determining whether a learner can carry out the task, determining the efficacy of the training materials, and providing a foundation for further levels of evaluation. Coscarelli and Shrock (2008) describe a five-step method for developing CRTs that include

1. Determining what to test (analysis)

2. Determining if the test measures what it purports to measure (validity)

3. Writing test items

4. Establishing a cut-off or mastery score

5. Showing that the test provides consistent results (reliability).

Level 3. Measuring the Results of Training Back on the Job

The next level of evaluation identifies whether the learning was actually used back on the job. It is important to recognize that application on the job is where learning actually begins to have real-world effects and that application is not solely up to the learner. Many elements affect transfer and application, including follow-up, manager support, and so forth. For example, consider a sales training attendee who attends training and learns a new, more efficient way to identify sales leads. However, upon returning to work, the attendee's manager does not allow the time for the attendee to practice applying those new skills in the workplace. Over time, the training is forgotten, and any value it may have had does not accrue.

Methods for collecting data regarding performance back on the job include reports by people who manage participants, reports from staff and peers, observations, quality monitors, and other quality and efficiency measures. In "The Four Levels of Evaluation," Don Kirkpatrick (2007) provides some guidelines for carrying out Level 3 evaluations:

- Use a control group, if practical.
- Allow time for behavior change to take place.
- Evaluate before and after the program, if possible.
- Interview learners, their immediate managers, and possibly their subordinates and anyone else who observes their work or behavior.
- Repeat the evaluation at appropriate times.

Level 4. Measuring the Organizational Impact of Training

Level 4 identifies how learning affects business measures. Consider an example related to management training. Let's say a manager attends management training and learns several new and valuable techniques to engage employees and help keep them on track. Upon return, the manager gets support in applying the new skills and behaviors. As time passes, the learning starts to have measurable results: Retention has increased, employees are demonstrably more engaged and are producing better-quality goods, and sales increase because the quality has increased. Retention, engagement, quality, and sales are all measurable business results improved as a result of the training.

Measuring such organizational impact requires working with leaders to create and implement a plan to collect the data you need. Possible methods include customer surveys, measurements of sales, studies of customer retention or turnover, employee satisfaction surveys, and other measurements of issues pertinent to the organization.

Robert Brinkerhoff, well-known author and researcher of evaluation methods, has suggested the following method to obtain information relevant to results:

- Send out questionnaires to people who have gone through training, asking: To what extent have you used your training in a way that has made a significant business impact? (This question can elicit information that will point to business benefits and ways to use other data to measure accomplishments.)
- When you get responses back, conduct interviews to get more information.

Return on Investment

Measuring return on investment (ROI)—sometimes referred to as Level 5 evaluation—is useful and can help "sell" training to leaders. ROI measures the monetary value of business benefits such as those noted in the discussion about Level 4 and compares them with the fully loaded costs of training to provide a percentage return on training investment. Hard numbers such as these can be helpful in discussions with organizational executives about conducting further training and raise the profile of training.

ROI was popularized by Jack Phillips. More in-depth information can be found in the *ASTD Handbook of Measuring and Evaluating Training* (Phillips 2010).

Reporting Results

An important and often under-considered component of both ROI and Level 4 evaluations is reporting results. Results from these types of evaluation studies have several different audiences, and it is important to take time to plan the layout of the evaluation report and the method of delivery with the audience in question. Consider the following tasks in preparing communications:

- **Purpose:** The purposes for communicating program results depend on the specific program, the setting, and unique organizational needs.
- **Audience:** For each target audience, understand the audience and find out what information is needed and why. Take into account audience bias, and then tailor the communication to each group.

- **Timing:** Lay the groundwork for communication before program implementation. Avoid delivering a message, particularly a negative message, to an audience unprepared to hear the story and unaware of the methods that generated the results.
- **Reporting format:** The type of formal evaluation report depends on how much detailed information is presented to target audiences. Brief summaries may be sufficient for some communication efforts. In other cases, particularly those programs that require significant funding, more detail may be important.

The Bare Minimum

- If formal measurement techniques are not possible, consider using the simple, interactive, informal measurement activities or a quick pulse-check during the workshop.
- Empower the participants to create an action plan to capture the new skills and ideas they plan to use. Ultimately, the success of any training event will rest on lasting positive change in participants' behavior.

Key Points

- The four basic levels of evaluation cover reaction, learning, application, and organizational impact.
- A fifth level covers return on investment.
- Reporting results is as important as measuring them. Be strategic in crafting your results document, taking into consideration purpose, audience, timing, and format.

What to Do Next

- Identify the purpose and level of evaluation based on the learning objectives and learning goals.
- Prepare a training evaluation form, or use the one provided in Chapter 14.
- If required, develop plans for follow-up evaluations to determine skills mastery, on-the-job application, and business impact.

Additional Resources

Biech, E., ed. (2014). *ASTD Handbook: The Definitive Reference for Training & Development,* 2nd edition. Alexandria, VA: ASTD Press.

Brinkerhoff, R.O. (2006). *Telling Training's Story: Evaluation Made Simple, Credible, and Effective.* San Francisco: Berrett-Koehler.

Coscarelli, W., and S. Shrock. (2008). "Level 2: Learning—Five Essential Steps for Creating Your Tests and Two Cautionary Tales." In E. Biech, ed., *ASTD Handbook for Workplace Learning Professionals*. Alexandria, VA: ASTD Press.

Kirkpatrick, D.L. (2007). "The Four Levels of Evaluation." *Infoline* No. 0701, Alexandria, VA: ASTD Press.

Kirkpatrick, D., and J.D. Kirkpatrick. (2006). *Evaluating Training Programs: The Four Levels,* 3rd edition. San Francisco: Berrett-Koehler.

Kirkpatrick, D., and J.D. Kirkpatrick. (2007). *Implementing the Four Levels: A Practical Guide for Effective Evaluation of Training Programs.* San Francisco: Berrett-Koehler.

Kristiansen, N.S. (2004). "Making Smile Sheets Count." *Infoline* No. 0402, Alexandria, VA: ASTD Press.

Phillips, P.P., ed. (2010). *ASTD Handbook of Measuring and Evaluating Training.* Alexandria, VA: ASTD Press.

SECTION III
POST-WORKSHOP LEARNING

Chapter 10
The Follow-Up Coach

What's in This Chapter

- Discerning what workshops can and can't do
- Setting the stage for follow-up
- Selling follow-up to leaders and stakeholders

> **TRAINING MANAGER:** What can we do to teach coaching skills?
>
> **TRAINER:** Let's offer a workshop.
>
> **TRAINING MANAGER:** Great. Workshops are helpful.
>
> **TRAINER:** But then what will we do to teach coaching skills?

You have likely learned this already, but the workshop is not *the* learning solution for any skills gap. It's not even the most important learning method—not by a long shot. Most learning occurs outside the workshop. This is especially true for coaching skills because becoming a great coach requires active practice. The workshops offered in this book are an important part of your learning solution for developing basic coaching skills—but, to reiterate, they play just a part.

Set the Stage for Post-Workshop Support

When other trainers share their learning plans with me, I make sure that they have spent more time planning the after-class activities than they have preparing for the workshop. Here are questions to help you create a great follow-up plan:

- What type of after-class actions will best reinforce and deepen the skills you are introducing to participants in the workshop? (Workshops only introduce topics and skills; the real learning comes much later.)

- How quickly will workshop participants hear from you? (Best answer? Less than a week.)

- How will you involve managers in reinforcing effective coaching skills?

- What opportunities for practice can you share and encourage?

- How will you continue to engage and *pull* participants into the topic of coaching so that they hone their craft?

- Which methods will you use to keep participants engaged?

- What will you tell participants will happen after the workshop?

Answering these questions will help you build a robust after-workshop plan that ensures that learning takes place. I don't like to say we are reinforcing the learning because that is misleading: When participants leave the classroom, the learning has *not yet occurred*. So, the after-workshop plan is needed to ensure learning happens.

Sell Post-Workshop Learning Activities to Leaders and Stakeholders

Many leaders like to think that building skills is a once-and-done endeavor. Send someone to a class, and presto-chango, he or she is competent. Budgets and time pressures drive this kind of thinking, but most leaders know in their gut that classroom training alone won't solve their performance gaps. Even so, training departments are often asked to accomplish skill development using only one of the tools from their toolbox.

So what should you do? My recommendation is that you come up with a simple after-workshop plan and then sell it to leaders. Many follow-up activities that leaders object to are overly burdensome to operations, so you must strive to continue the learning in ways that are operationally feasible. Here are some examples:

- Use existing meeting structures (such as huddles, team meetings, and staff meetings) to share additional information and conduct short skills practices.

- Work with coaches in pairs or trios for short bursts of time (ideally 30 minutes or less).

- Offer to provide coaching for coaches as they prepare for a coaching session (just-in-time equals relevant coaching).

- Choose reading material or videos that are short and accessible by all participants. (Don't require participants to log in from home—I once knew a company that did this because most Internet access was blocked at work.)
- Design post-workshop practice opportunities that directly relate to daily work or upcoming projects.

Make sure your plan speaks the language of your business and indicates that you understand people's jobs and priorities to get commitment and support from leaders. And better yet, help them see the virtues of great coaching and turn them into evangelists for development!

Enjoy Post-Workshop Learning

Personally, I find the more hand-crafted learning activities that often occur *after* classroom training more fun and creative. It's a challenge to determine how to best keep participants engaged, and it requires that we walk our talk and engage in great conversations until we build solid relationships and connections. It's a time when we can use our coaching skills to help others succeed. In the next chapter, I will share a few more specific ideas for after-workshop learning activities.

The Bare Minimum

- Remember that growing coaching skills is a journey—not an event. Most learning occurs outside the workshop.
- Be creative and consistent. Engage participants in great conversations until they are able to do the same for others.
- Follow-up, with multiple offerings, helps learners implement their action plans and make real progress toward improving behavior and achieving results.
- Management involvement, though difficult to get at first, is critical to organizational change, and so you will need to "sell" follow-up activities to leaders and stakeholders.

What to Do Next

- Select one or two of the follow-up ideas and make a plan to implement them in your next workshop. Use the questions presented earlier in this chapter to help you build a robust after-workshop plan.
- Follow through on your follow-up plan. Demonstrate your commitment to your participants' continued learning by your willingness to continue on the journey with them long after the workshop is completed.

Chapter 11
Follow-Up Activities

What's in This Chapter

- Timing follow-up
- Becoming a matchmaker
- Using technology to support follow-up activities
- Building in coaching community
- Measuring post-workshop activities

Coaching skills are developed slowly and through practice—a learning continuum of sorts. Because coaching occurs in conversations, most of your after-class activities will involve discussions (even if virtual). This means that to build coaching capability at your workplace, you will need to have an after-workshop plan that makes connections between coaches and performers consistently and over time.

Don't Wait to Follow Up

Wait no longer than a week to reach out to workshop participants before their mile-long to-do lists have taken priority, and coaching retreats far from their minds. Right after the class is an excellent time to offer a short and interesting email that shares a story about coaching and offers 10 ways they can work more coaching into their busy work schedules. Tailor this email to your industry because the typical excuses for not coaching might be unique (or at least participants might think they are). Consider including a quick two-item survey embedded right into the email to get some feedback.

Another option is to enlist one of the senior leaders to send an email that praises the value of coaching and encourages participants to seek opportunities to use coaching. At one large company, for example, I worked with the CEO to record a quick video congratulating participants on finishing the workshop and asking them now to use what they learned. The participants were not expecting this, and it was a nice surprise.

Practice, Practice, Practice

I would like you to expand your definition of practice. Practicing full-length coaching sessions is extremely valuable, but you can also help coaches learn their craft in smaller practice sessions. I have done 10-minute practice sessions as a regular part of team meetings. I have facilitated 30- and 60-minute lunch-and-learn sessions that were 10 percent content, 90 percent practice. Remember the pairs exercises that were part of the workshop (where participants checked a couple of boxes, switched worksheets, and practiced)? You can do facilitated practice sessions like these in as little as 20 minutes. They're fun and they work. Practice is very important and should make up at least one-third of your after-workshop activities.

Be a Matchmaker

Coaching requires two people: the coach and the performer. Take the initiative to find and match up performers with coaches. I love this idea and use it often. When co-workers share their goals and frustrations, I say, "I bet you could make some real progress if you could talk through your goals and plan with a coach. How about I set that up? It will only take an hour, and you're not making a commitment beyond that." The nice thing about the daily coaching model presented in this book is that using it does not require that coaches and performers make long-term commitments to meet a certain number of times over a certain number of months. Some of the best coaching I have ever received lasted less than an hour total. You can help make these magical hours happen more often.

Use Technology

Technology solutions can help keep the topic of coaching fresh for participants and help them explore some of the more complex concepts with after-workshop mini-sessions. For example, the idea of creating pull will likely resonate with workshop participants, but the workshop may not have spent enough time on it to make the topic crystal clear. This would be an excellent topic for a mini-session, and there are many others. Use webinars or video conferencing to connect with coaches, share content, and encourage discussion.

As discussed in Chapter 7, here are some ideas for using technology after the workshop to increase engagement, deepen understanding, and increase application:

- *To increase engagement:* Learners engage when they perceive something as interesting, relevant right now, or challenging. Use tools such as video, blogs, social networks, chat, websites, and email to increase interest in the topic and to provide challenge.

- *To deepen understanding:* Use after-workshop surveys and polling tools to assess understanding so you can address any gap. Add to the participants' understanding of the topic by posting materials on a SharePoint site or through blog posts that you push to their email inboxes using an RSS feed.

- *To increase application:* Provide a just-in-time online resource where participants find quick reference sheets and get application tips using a group site, social network, or SharePoint site. Request or require that participants report how they have used new skills through an online project management collaboration site, wiki, or email group.

Ask participants which of these or other methods would best meet their needs and help them stay engaged.

Build a Coaching Community

In an ideal world, coaches learn from each other, shifting back and forth between the role of coach and performer. This builds connection and helps coaching succeed. Creating a pro-coaching community will reduce uncoachability triggers, which in turn will serve the organization very well. When coaches practice and learn from each other, their defenses and fears diminish and coachability soars. Have you ever noticed that you see all the cars that look like yours on the highway? We recognize and pull into what we know and select. And when we coach more and talk about coaching skills in a safe environment, we see coaching in a more favorable light overall—and we seek it for ourselves.

Technology can be a great asset in building community. Busy people value community but often can't make the time to attend follow-up sessions or network with peers. They might, however, be able to take 10 minutes to check in on an internal social network, group site, or blog to learn from and share with others. If your organization does not have social networking or collaboration software, you might need to get creative. Talk to your technology department about the tools you have—whether they are SharePoint, blog software, internal messaging, a wiki-type project management collaboration tool, or other. You can even use email groups to connect learners. Look for ways you can create *pull* (they choose when to engage) and *push* (they get updates, such as using RSS feeds).

Use a collaborative online project site or social network to set expectations about post-workshop peer discussions and reinforce engagement. Poll participants and assign sub-teams to lead a portion of each web meeting.

Coaching occurs in conversations, and you can enable excellent virtual discussions by using technology to connect coaches and encourage sharing of best practices and experiences.

Measure Post-Workshop Activities

Chapter 9 focuses on the art of measuring training effectiveness, so I won't go into this topic here. I might, however, contradict the idea that you need to measure all aspects of your training plan. When it comes to after-workshop activities, make sure that you are focusing on the right goal. Everything you do should be aimed at increasing coaching frequency and effectiveness. Some of the actions I have suggested are not easy to measure, and I wouldn't want this to scare you away from doing them. For example, you can't measure the learning transfer of a 10-minute practice session done as part of a staff meeting, and you won't likely know the real impact of pairing up performers and coaches on an ad hoc basis. But they are still the right things to do. There is no quicker way to encourage and enhance coaching than to make it a part of what's happening in the work stream. Measure what you can and then do great work because you know that it will add up and make a positive difference.

The Bare Minimum

- **Try Many Ways to Keep Participants Interested, Active, and Engaged.** Hone your after-workshop activities until you have a well-oiled learning machine ready to continue what you started in the workshop.

- **Grit = Success.** Don't give up when you face resistance, meetings are cancelled, or you discover that only five people have viewed the recorded webinar that took you 10 hours to create. Stick with it and take notice of the activities that participants pull into. Do more of those!

- **Practice, Practice, Practice.** Expand your idea of practice to include short, mini-practice sessions as part of regular team meetings or lunch-and-learns.

What to Do Next

- **Start implementing your follow-up plan immediately after the workshop.** Don't wait until busy workplace schedules overwhelm their priorities.

- **Leverage technology to continue the learning.** Pick at least one follow-up activity that uses technology as its delivery medium. Technology solutions can provide effective and affordable tools for your follow-up tool kit.

- **Play matchmaker.** Find and match up coaches and performers. The daily coaching model presented in this book can be effective in short bursts on short notice in many formal and informal coaching conversations.

- **Create a pro-coaching community.** Look for ways to create *pull*.

SECTION IV

WORKSHOP SUPPORTING DOCUMENTS AND ONLINE SUPPORT

Chapter 12
Learning Activities

What's in This Chapter

- Fifteen learning activities to use in your workshops

- Complete step-by-step instructions for each activity

- Handouts and graphics needed to facilitate the activities located in Chapter 14

- Refer to Chapter 15 for instructions to download full-size handouts

To help you facilitate adult learning, we have designed learning activities to deploy regularly throughout the workshop. Their purpose is to challenge and engage learners by breaking up monotony, providing stimulation for different types of learners, and actively helping them acquire new knowledge. Such activities enliven and invigorate the experience, and they help learning "stick."

Each learning activity provides detailed information about learning objectives, materials required, timeframe, step-by-step instructions, and variations and debriefing questions if required. Follow the instructions in each learning activity to prepare your workshop agenda, identify and gather materials needed, and successfully guide learners through the activity. The experiences provided by the learning activities help support the topics covered in the workshop. See Chapter 15 for complete instructions on how to download the workshop support materials.

You might find that some of the learning activities are simple and straightforward enough that you prefer to put the facilitator instructions in the three-column agendas in Chapters 1-3. For consistency sake, we have included all learning activities here. Each learning activity is structured to provide this information:

- Objective: Overall purpose of the activity
- Materials: What you will need to conduct the activity

- Time: How long the activity should take

- Instructions: Detailed steps to facilitate the activity

- Discussion Questions for Debriefing: Question prompts to help participants transfer their learning.

Learning Activities Included in *Coaching Training*

Learning Activity 1: My Coaching Story

Learning Activity 2: What Does Coaching Feel Like?

Learning Activity 3: Coaching Skills Diagnostic

Learning Activity 4: Listen Deeply

Learning Activity 5: Coachability Scenarios

Learning Activity 6: Uncoachability Triggers

Learning Activity 7: Ways to Offer Coaching

Learning Activity 8: Day-Two Warm-Up

Learning Activity 9: Creating Pull

Learning Activity 10: Ask Better Questions

Learning Activity 11: First Practice Coaching Session

Learning Activity 12: Critical Thinking Exercise

Learning Activity 13: Final Practice Coaching Session

Learning Activity 14: Getting Started and Asking Great Questions

Learning Activity 15: Quick Start to Critical Thinking

Learning Activity 1: My Coaching Story

LEARNING ACTIVITY 1

My Coaching Story

Objectives

Participants will be able to

- Explore coaching by self-identifying when they have provided or received coaching and share questions they have about coaching
- Provide facilitator with a baseline regarding the group's overall experience level.

Materials

- Presentation Slide 4
- Two flipcharts
- Markers
- Sticky notes
- Pens

Time

35 minutes

Instructions

1. Place two flipcharts on easels in the front of the room (or use large "sticky note" chart paper on the front wall). Write "Goal" on the top of one and "Burning Question" on the other.

2. Divide participants into groups of 4 to 6 (at their tables). Tell participants that you will be using this warm-up activity to get a feel for their coaching experience and to help them to get to know their tablemates.

3. Give each person two sticky notes and a pen. Ask participants to write "Goal" on the top of one note and "Burning Question" on the top of the other.

Learning Activity 1, *continued*

4. Instruct participants to start their group discussion by introducing themselves and then answering the questions on the slide (about 15 minutes). Ask the participants to think about their personal coaching story, including their experiences giving and receiving coaching or their impression of coaching. Ask them to identify a goal they would like to discuss with a coach and a burning question related to coaching and then to write the goal and the question on the respective sticky note.

5. Once everyone has completed their introductions and shared their responses, direct them to come up to the front of the room and place their two sticky notes on the corresponding flipchart.

6. Move into a 10-minute group debrief using the questions below. Let them know that you will be referring back to the flipcharts throughout the workshop (and do so).

Discussion Questions for Debriefing

- Was it difficult to answer any of the questions? Which one? Why?
- Did you notice any themes emerge as each person shared their experiences and responses?
- Let's look at what's on the flipcharts. (Read them aloud quickly.) What themes do you identify?
- Should everyone have a goal they would like to discuss with a coach?

Learning Activity 2: What Does Coaching Feel Like?

LEARNING ACTIVITY 2

What Does Coaching Feel Like?

Objectives

Participants will be able to

- Think from the point of view of the performer so that they will be better able to provide coaching that is well received and welcomed by the performer
- Reflect on their experience as performers and consider whether they have experienced service-oriented coaching (many have never received coaching like this)
- Distinguish coaching as defined in this workshop from other helpful conversations often confused with coaching.

Materials

- Presentation Slide 18
- Flipchart
- Sticky notes
- Pens

Time

30 minutes

Instructions

This activity is straightforward but might feel difficult for participants at first. Confirm that participants now understand what coaching is and how it differs from other conversations often confused with coaching. Based on this new understanding, you want them to reflect on whether they have experienced coaching, and if so, how it felt to receive it. Note that many participants will report they can't think of a time they received coaching as you have defined it. Encourage them to imagine what it would feel like to receive great coaching.

Learning Activity 2, *continued*

1. Place a flipchart in front of room (or use large "sticky note" chart paper on the front wall). Label the chart "What Does Coaching Feel Like?"

2. Divide participants into discussion teams of two or three.

3. Ask participants to take 10 minutes to answer and discuss the following question: "Think about the last time you received coaching the way we have defined it. What did it feel like? If you cannot recall coaching you have received, imagine what it would feel like."

4. Instruct participants to write their responses to this question on a sticky note and then post on the chart.

5. Ask each group to share an example of how it felt to receive coaching as defined in this workshop. If you have more than 10 discussion teams, consider just sharing an example of your own.

6. Lead a short group discussion with the questions below to debrief the activity.

Discussion Questions for Debriefing

- What's the key difference between how coaching feels to receive versus how advice feels to receive?
- Does everyone deserve to be served in the way we are describing as great coaching?
- How many of you feel a bit intimidated by how we have defined coaching? (Let them know that's why they are here—to become more comfortable delivering great coaching.)
- How many of you would welcome great coaching, as we have defined it?

Learning Activity 3: Coaching Skills Diagnostic

Coaching Skills Diagnostic

Objectives

Participants will be able to

- Complete the coaching skills diagnostic and then discuss the results in a small group setting
- Reflect on their experience as performers and consider whether they have experienced service-oriented coaching (many have never received coaching like this)
- Gain a baseline view of their coaching skills in relation to the model presented in this workshop.

Materials

- Presentation Slide 19
- Assessment 1: Coaching Skills Diagnostic

Time

45 minutes

Instructions

This activity is conducted before presenting the coaching model to promote deeper listening and to enable participants to apply what they learn specifically to the area in which they most need to improve

1. Distribute Assessment 1: Coaching Skills Diagnostic and go over the instructions with the participants. Ask them to read through each item and place an "X" in either the "Hmm... I need to work on" or "Strength: I got this!" column based on their self-assessment. Let participants know that it is natural that they will self-assess several items as "Hmm... I need to work on." This is not an easy assessment to "ace." Ask them to consider each item fully. There are no scores, and nothing will be collected.

Learning Activity 3, *continued*

2. Once they have assessed all the items, direct them to review the entire assessment and then select two or three items that are most interesting to them (that is, have the most pull for them). Their "My Focus Few" can come from items rated as either strengths or weaknesses. Allow 20 minutes to complete the assessment.

3. After the 20 minutes is over, ask participants to share briefly what they thought of the assessment.

4. Then direct participants to share their overall impression of their coaching skills in their table groups. Ask them to discuss what they feel are their strengths, which items made them cringe a bit, and so on. Allow 15 minutes for the group discussion (about 3 minutes per person).

5. Debrief the assessment for the remaining 5 minutes using the discussion questions below.

Discussion Questions for Debriefing

- How many of you found this assessment hard?
- What do these assessment items tell you about what it means to provide great coaching?
- Were there any questions that surprised you? Which ones and why?

Learning Activity 4: Listen Deeply

Listen Deeply

Objectives

Participants will be able to

- Rehearse showing interest in others and giving others their full attention
- Practice deep listening so that they can distinguish it from active listening or partial listening, which are more common in the workplace.

Materials

- Presentation Slides 25-26 (Two-Day Workshop)
- Presentation Slides 16-17 (One-Day Workshop)
- Presentation Slides 34-35 (Half-Day Workshop)

Time

20 minutes

Instructions

This exercise is deceptively simple. The listener's job is to honestly become interested in what the speaker is saying. To listen deeply is to show interest and to take in what the speaker is saying without distraction.

1. Divide the participants into pairs (use one trio if there is an odd number).

2. Review the instructions on slide with the participants. There is no preparation time required because everyone can think of and share a favorite hobby (ask participants to select a hobby that is suitable for sharing in a professional setting; they will laugh at this).

3. Ask each pair to select who will go first. That person will be in the role of the speaker and will talk about a hobby he or she loves and why. The other participant is the listener (two listeners if you have a trio).

Learning Activity 4, *continued*

4. The listener's job is to become honestly interested in what the speaker is sharing. If the speaker stops talking, the listener is to ask a question so he or she can learn more about the hobby and why the speaker loves it. Speakers should do 90 percent of the talking; listeners should ensure they do not become distracted from the conversation. Listeners need to keep speakers talking for 5 minutes, and they should listen deeply the entire time.

5. After 5 minutes, ask the pairs to switch roles and rerun the activity. The second speaker will speak for 5 minutes, with the listener listening deeply. The pair is not to switch roles until after the 5 minutes are up.

6. Debrief the assessment for the remaining 5 minutes using the discussion questions below.

Discussion Questions for Debriefing

- What does it feel like to be listened to in this way?
- What does it feel like to listen in this way?

Learning Activity 5: Coachability Scenarios

Coachability Scenarios

Objectives

Participants will be able to

- Define and understand the concept of coachability
- Gain ideas for how to improve coachability back in their workplace by exploring common scenarios.

Materials

- Presentation Slides 45-47 (Two-Day Wworkshop)
- Presentation slide 31 (One-Day Workshop)

Time

60 minutes (Two-Day Workshop)

10 minutes (One-Day Workshop)

Instructions

Coachability is not a commonly held idea, so offering examples of what it might look like will help performers to open up.

Two-Day Workshop

1. Direct participants to work together in their table groups (4-6 people).
2. For each of the three scenarios, review the scenario and discussion question on the slide with the participants.

Learning Activity 5, *continued*

3. Ask each table to discuss each of the scenarios and questions for 10 minutes and then define three ways they might improve the performer's coachability.
4. Process each scenario for 5-8 minutes, asking table groups to share one of their ideas.
5. Debrief as a group using the questions below.

One-Day Workshop

1. Review the scenario and question on the slide.
2. Lead a group discussion of the scenario and the participants' responses to the question for 10 minutes. Ask participants to define three ways they might improve the coachability of the performer in the scenario.
3. Debrief as a group using the questions below.

Discussion Questions for Debriefing

- Were these scenarios realistic? Have you known people like this?
- Might you share any of these triggers and would the ideas you generated work on you?

Learning Activity 6: Uncoachability Triggers

Uncoachability Triggers

Objectives

Participants will be able to

- Improve their awareness of situations that tend to most affect their coachability
- Acknowledge their triggers so that they can better catch and prevent themselves from becoming uncoachable.

Materials

- Presentation Slide 48 (Two-Day Workshop)
- Presentation Slide 32 (One-Day Workshop)
- Presentation Slide 37 (Half-Day Workshop)
- Assessment 2: Uncoachability Triggers Checklist

Time

15 minutes

Instructions

1. Distribute Assessment 2: Uncoachability Triggers Checklist. Review the instructions on the slide and the handout. The checklist presents common triggers that reduce coachability for some people, some of the time. Ask participants to check any item that has impacted their coachability in the last month. If they can't recall a specific situation from the last month, check off the triggers that they know can affect whether they seek or hear coaching or input. Give participants up to 5 minutes to complete the checklist.

Learning Activity 6, *continued*

2. Tell participants that it is normal to check off several triggers. The purpose of this exercise is to help them recognize common triggers so that they can catch themselves as they are becoming less coachable and choose a more open stance.
3. Ask, by show of hands, how many triggers they checked off, starting with 5, then 7, then 10 or more.
4. Ask them to share with their table groups the situation that most often triggers their uncoachability and why. (5 minutes)
5. Share one of your own triggers. Encourage participants to notice their triggers and then choose a more open stance. Remind them that being more aware of triggers helps coaches provide an environment that improves performer coachability. Knowledge is power!
6. Debrief by discussing the questions below.

Discussion Questions for Debriefing

- Can you stop yourself from becoming uncoachable? (The answer is yes.)
- What themes did you notice about the triggers you checked off? In which category did you check off the most triggers?
- What does this exercise tell you regarding ways you might be able to help improve performer coachability?

Learning Activity 7: Ways to Offer Coaching

Ways to Offer Coaching

Objectives

Participants will be able to learn and practice ways to start a coaching conversation.

Materials

- Presentation Slide 51
- Paper and pens

Time

20-25 minutes

Instructions

Coaches might resist offering coaching because they aren't comfortable beginning the conversation, so it is important that they practice starting coaching conversations. This exercise builds on the coachability discussion.

1. Divide the participants into work groups of 2 or 3 people (groups of 4 people are fine if you have more than 20 participants).

2. Based on what they now know about coachability, ask participants how they can offer coaching in ways that will engage the performer (versus make them uncomfortable)?

3. Ask each group to create three opening lines they might use to offer coaching. The goal is to offer coaching in ways that encourage performer ownership and enhance performer coachability.

Original material by Lisa Haneberg, © 2016 Association for Talent Development (ATD). Used with permission. COACHING training 1

Learning Activity 7, *continued*

4. Direct each group to perform their opening lines (about 10 minutes total, with each group simply sharing three opening lines).

5. Debrief the activity by discussing the questions below for 5 minutes.

Discussion Questions for Debriefing

- Which opening line appealed to you?

- Is it hard to offer coaching? Why? What "story" are you telling yourself about coaching?

Original material by Lisa Haneberg, © 2016 Association for Talent Development (ATD). Used with permission. COACHING training 2

Learning Activity 8: Day-Two Warm-Up

Day-Two Warm-Up

Objectives

Participants will be able to

- Reflect on the previous day's learning
- Distinguish something new about coaching.

Materials

- Presentation Slide 65

Time

20 minutes

Instructions

1. Divide the group into teams of 2 to 4 people.

2. Give teams 10 minutes to answer two questions presented on slide: What is the most useful thing you learned during yesterday's class? How has your perception about coaching changed?

3. Process the warm-up by having each team share one example response (10 minutes). Lead a group discussion using the debriefing questions below.

Discussion Questions for Debriefing

- As a result of our discussion yesterday, are you more or less interested in coaching others?

- Did you notice anything that triggered your uncoachability after you left the session yesterday (perhaps with family members or friends)?

Original material by Lisa Haneberg, © 2016 Association for Talent Development (ATD). Used with permission. COACHING training

Learning Activity 9: Creating Pull

Creating Pull

Objectives

Participants will be able to learn and explore ways to increase performer engagement and ownership through techniques that use pull rather than push practices.

Materials

- Presentation Slide 70 (Two-Day Workshop)
- Presentation Slide 38 (One-Day Workshop)
- Presentation Slide 39 (Half-Day Workshop)
- Handout 3: Conversation Characteristics That Create Pull
- Blank flipchart paper and markers

Time

40 minutes (Two-Day Workshop)

10-15 minutes (One-Day and Half-Day Workshops)

Instructions

1. Pass out Handout 3 to participants. Ask them to work with their table groups to use the conversation characteristics on the handout to help them brainstorm 10 ways to increase pull in coaching conversations. Let them know that they will be asked to share their entire list later in the activity.

2. Remind them to be specific: for example, "Be Fascinating" is not specific enough. Direct them to think of a few specific strategies they could use to increase fascination in a typical coaching discussion. Be prepared to share an example of a strategy: "Share something you learned from a provocative article that relates to the performer's goal." The types of things they should be coming up with can relate to the setting, adding fun or drama, introducing people and making connections, mapping out the plan, celebrating milestones, and so on.

Original material by Lisa Haneberg, © 2016 Association for Talent Development (ATD). Used with permission. COACHING training 1

Learning Activity 9, continued

3. Give teams 10-15 minutes (two-day) or 5 minutes (one- and half-day) to complete their list of 10 ideas.

4. When teams have completed their lists, ask them to read their ideas aloud to the whole group. As they do, chart their answers in summarized form ("celebrate milestones") on the flipchart in the front of the room labeled "Ways to Increase Pull in Conversations." Use several sheets of chart paper if needed and post them on the wall. Continue to record the ideas until all the groups have shared their ideas.

5. Then ask for any additional ideas from the entire group, putting checkmarks next to repeat answers. Reflect on the number of ways coaches can help increase pull and the benefits of taking the time to try. For one- and half-day agendas, skip step 5 and go directly to step 6.

6. Debrief the activity by leading a discussion of the questions below.

Discussion Questions for Debriefing

- Which of these ideas would most appeal to you if you were the performer? Why?

- Could you use these techniques to create more pull in a group or small team setting?

Learning Activity 10: Ask Better Questions

Ask Better Questions

Objectives

Participants will be able to practice creating and asking great questions.

Materials

- Presentation Slide 76

Time

15 minutes

Instructions

1. Direct participants to work with their table groups to complete this activity.

2. Review the instructions on the slide with the participants. Ask them to imagine that they are coaching John, who is frustrated with the pace of progress on a project that means a lot to him. Ask teams to brainstorm in their groups to come up with three great questions that might help John explore his situation and make progress (5 minutes). Let them know you will ask for at least one example from every table.

3. Ask teams to share their best question with the entire group.

4. Give feedback along the way. Reinforce for the participants that great questions shape the discussion and open up a performer's thinking.

5. Debrief the activity by discussing the questions below.

Learning Activity 10, continued

Discussion Questions for Debriefing

- What did you notice about these questions? Were they open or closed?

- Is it OK to challenge performers with a tough question?

- What type of questions might you want to avoid? (For example, questions that are critical/judging, pessimistic, assumptive/too easy, leading, or take the discussion off topic should be avoided.)

Learning Activity 11: First Practice Coaching Session

First Practice Coaching Session

Objectives

Participants will be able to

- Experience what it is like to give and receive coaching as defined in this course

- Practice starting the coaching conversation, listening deeply, creating pull, and asking great questions.

Materials

- Presentation Slide 79 (Two-Day Workshop)
- Presentation Slide 44 (One-Day Workshop)
- Handout 4: My Coaching Worksheet
- Handout 5: Practice 1 Coaching Worksheet
- Handout 2: Coaching Roles

Time

60 minutes

Instructions

This activity, Coaching Practice 1, provides participants the opportunity to practice starting the coaching conversation, listening deeply, creating pull, and asking great questions. Coaching Practice 2 later in the workshop will add more elements of the coaching model.

1. Pass out Handout 4: My Coaching Worksheet and ask participants to pull out Handout 2: Coaching Roles from earlier in the workshop. Go over the items to be completed and then ask each person to take 5 minutes to complete Handout 4, which will help them prepare for the coaching exercise. Offer to answer questions, but as long as they identify a real topic they are interested in, they will be fine.

Learning Activity 11, *continued*

2. After participants have completed Handout 4, divide them into pairs. If you have an odd number of participants you can use one trio (with one person observing each round and 10-minute instead of 15-minute rounds), or you can use the co-facilitator as a participant if you are team-facilitating this course. Consider mixing up pairs so that they can work with someone they have not yet worked with in the workshop. This activity can be conducted with pairs sitting side by side at tables, standing (they will need something hard to write on such as a binder or book), or pulling two chairs together.

3. Ask pair partners to switch Handout 4 with each other so that they are looking at their partner's sheet. (Note: if you have one group of three, have them pass their handouts to their right.)

4. Pass out Handout 5: Practice 1 Coaching Worksheet to each person and quickly review the items on the sheet. Give each person 10 minutes to fill out handout to prepare for the coaching conversation. Ask them not to start talking or coaching until you say "start."

5. **Coaching Round 1:** After participants have completed preparation with Handout 5, ask each pair to determine who goes first (person with the brightest shirt or tallest person). Review the roles quickly. Emphasize that coaches should do whatever they can to honestly help; their job is to listen deeply, create pull, and ask good questions. The performers need to remain coachable and seek the coaching. This is a real coaching session (or the start of one). Tell each pair they have 15 minutes for this round and ask them to start. Announce when 5 minutes, 10 minutes, and 13 minutes have passed. Stop them at 15 minutes.

6. **Coaching Round 2:** Ask partners to switch roles. Tell each pair they have 15 minutes for this second round and ask them to start. Announce when 5 minutes, 10 minutes, and 13 minutes have passed. Stop them at 15 minutes. Ask each person to return Handout 4 to the performer and return to their table seats.

7. Don't take too much time to process this activity because the second coaching practice later in workshop will continue to build their skills in more depth. For now, ask for general reactions—how it felt to give and receive the coaching. Reinforce that while the coaching conversation was highly imperfect, it was still helpful. This is the way it will be in real coaching situations (and they will become more comfortable over time).

8. Discuss the activity briefly by using the debriefing questions below.

Learning Activity 11, *continued*

LEARNING ACTIVITY 11, continued

Discussion Questions for Debriefing

- Did you get some great coaching?
- What was it like, as the performer, to determine what you wanted to talk about?
- What was most difficult for you when you played the role of the coach?

Learning Activity 12: Critical Thinking Exercise

Critical Thinking Exercise

Objectives

Participants will be able to

- Identify common questions they can ask to help performers expand their perspectives
- Practice using these critical thinking questions in a coaching discussion.

Materials

- Presentation Slides 85-86 (Two-Day Workshop)
- Presentation Slide 40 (Half-Day Workshop)
- Handout 6: Critical Thinking Worksheet

Time

40 minutes

Instructions

1. Divide the group into pairs (with one trio if you have an odd number of participants). You can pair people up with folks at their table so they don't have to move.

2. Pass out Handout 6: Critical Thinking Worksheet to the participants and go over the top portion for performers. Ask each person to complete the "performer" portion. This should take just a minute or two.

3. Go over the remaining items on the worksheet and ask pairs to switch sheets. Ask each pair to determine who will be the coach and who will be the performer.

4. Direct each coach to interview the performer using these questions on the worksheet. The coach should take notes on the worksheet for the performer. Each round of interviews is 10 minutes, so let participants know when 5, 7, and 10 minutes have passed.

Learning Activity 12, *continued*

5. Then ask partners to switch roles and repeat process in step 5. Once the two rounds of interviews are complete, ask pairs to return handouts so that each performer has his or her sheet back with notes from the conversation.

6. Take about 15 minutes to process the activity. Use the questions on slide (two-day) and below to help guide your discussion.

Discussion Questions for Debriefing

- Did you find that these questions helped you expand your thinking about your problem or challenge? Why or why not?
- Which question was most helpful to you? (You can take a poll, asking them to raise hands so they see that each person might need a different question.)
- If a peer asked you these same questions tomorrow, would you remain coachable? (Some might find these questions challenging and get defensive, so this question is good to explore.)
- If you would like your team members to do more peer-level coaching, might you want to use this exercise at your next staff meeting? What's the downside? (The upside is that by making it an exercise, you might reduce the angst of the inquiry and increase coachability.)

Learning Activity 13: Final Practice Coaching Session

LEARNING ACTIVITY 13

Final Practice Coaching Session

Objectives

Participants will be able to practice delivering a real coaching session that requires them, as coaches, to listen deeply, create pull, ask great questions, improve coachability, provide perspective, and ensure performer progress.

Materials

- Presentation Slide 96 (Two-Day Workshop)
- Presentation Slide 61 (One-Day Workshop)
- Presentation Slide 44 (Half-Day Workshop)
- Handout 4: My Coaching Worksheet
- Handout 7: Practice 2 Coaching Worksheet (a two-page handout to be photocopied two-sided)
- Handout 2: Coaching Roles

Time

90 minutes (Two-Day Workshop)
55-60 minutes (One-Day and Half-Day Workshops)

Instructions

The shorter version of this activity used for the One-Day and Half-Day Workshops provides the same amount of coaching practice time but less debriefing time. You can choose to shorten the coaching time by 5 minutes each round if you want to build in more debriefing time.

Original material by Lisa Haneberg, © 2015 Association for Talent Development (ATD). Used with permission.

COACHING training 1

Learning Activity 13, *continued*

LEARNING ACTIVITY 13, continued

1. Ask participants to pull out Handout 2: Coaching Roles they used earlier in the workshop. Pass out Handout 4: My Coaching Worksheet to each participant. Participants can use the same Handout 6 they used for Coaching Practice 1). Go over the items on the worksheet and then ask each person to take 5 minutes to complete it. (Offer to answer questions, but as long as they identify a real topic they are interested in, it will work fine.)

2. Divide the participants into new pairs (someone they haven't worked with previously in the workshop). If you have an odd number of participants you can use one trio (with one person observing each round and 13-minute instead of 20-minute rounds), or you can use the co-facilitator as a participant if you are team-facilitating this course. This activity can be conducted with pairs sitting side by side at tables, standing (they will need something hard to write on such as a binder or book), or pulling two chairs together.

3. Ask pair partners to switch Handout 4 with each other so they are looking at their partner's sheet. (Note: if you have one group of three, have them pass their handouts to their right.)

4. Pass out Handout 7: Practice 2 Coaching Worksheet to each person and quickly review the items on the sheet. Give each person 15 minutes (two-day) or 10 minutes (one-day and half-day) to use this worksheet to prepare for the coaching conversation. This might seem like a long time for folks, but ask them to take the time to prepare. This is their final "exam" for the workshop, and it is real coaching. Ask them not to start talking or coaching until you say "start."

5. **Coaching Round 1:** After participants have completed preparation with Handout 7, ask each pair to determine who goes first (person with the most pets or whose birthday is closest to this date). Review the roles quickly. Emphasize that coaches should do whatever they can to honestly help; their job is to listen deeply, create pull, ask good questions, enhance coachability, provide perspective, and make progress. The performers' job is to remain coachable, seek the coaching, and be fully engaged. Tell each pair they have 20 minutes for this round and ask them to start. Announce when 5, 10, 15, and 18 minutes have passed. Stop them at 20 minutes.

6. **Coaching Round 2:** Ask partners to switch roles. Tell each pair they have 15 minutes for this second round and ask them to start. Announce when 5, 10, 15, and 18 minutes have

Original material by Lisa Haneberg, © 2015 Association for Talent Development (ATD). Used with permission.

COACHING training 2

Learning Activity 13, *continued*

LEARNING ACTIVITY 13, continued

passed. Stop them at 20 minutes. Ask each person to return Handout 4 to the performer and return to their table seats.

7. To help participants process this exercise, pulse the group for how they think the coaching sessions went. Use the debriefing questions below to lead the conversation.

Discussion Questions for Debriefing

- What did your coach do that really worked for you—that pulled you in?
- How could you use these planning worksheets for coaching sessions back on the job?
- What aspect of this practice was most difficult for you? Why?

Original material by Lisa Haneberg, © 2015 Association for Talent Development (ATD). Used with permission.

COACHING training 3

Learning Activity 14: Getting Started and Asking Great Questions

LEARNING ACTIVITY 14

Getting Started and Asking Great Questions

Objectives

Participants will be able to practice starting a coaching conversation and asking great questions (covering the first half of a typical coaching discussion).

Materials

- Presentation Slide 46
- Handout 8: Getting Started Practice Worksheet

Time

30 minutes

Instructions

1. Break the groups into pairs. If you have an odd number of participants you can use one trio (with one person observing each round and 7-minute instead of 10-minute rounds), or you can use the co-facilitator as a participant if you are team-facilitating this course. They can do this activity sitting side by side at tables, standing (they will need something hard to write on such as a binder or book), or pulling two chairs together.

2. Pass out Handout 8: Getting Started Practice Worksheet to each participant. Ask everyone to circle the item in the first portion of the worksheet that most appeals to them (you will notice that the worksheet contains several common goals or challenges). This should not take more than a minute or two.

3. Ask pairs to switch worksheets so they are looking at their partner's sheet. (Note: if you have one group of three, have each person pass their worksheet to their right.) Quickly review the items in the "coach" portion of the worksheet. Give each person 3 minutes to prepare for the coaching conversation. Ask participants not to start talking or coaching until you say "start."

Original material by Lisa Haneberg, © 2015 Association for Talent Development (ATD). Used with permission.

COACHING training 1

Learning Activity 14, *continued*

LEARNING ACTIVITY 14, continued

4. **Coaching Round 1:** After 3 minutes of planning, ask each pair to determine who goes first (person who lives closest to work or person who was born farthest away). Review the roles quickly. Emphasize that coaches should do whatever they can to honestly help; their job is to listen deeply, create pull, and ask good questions. The performers' job is to remain coachable, seek the coaching, and be fully engaged. This is a real coaching session. Tell each pair they have 10 minutes for this round and ask them to start. Announce when 5 and 8 minutes have passed. Stop them at 10 minutes.

5. **Coaching Round 2:** Ask partner pairs to switch roles. Tell each pair they have 10 minutes for this round and ask them to start. Announce when 5 and 8 minutes have passed. Stop them at 10 minutes.

6. To help participants process the exercise, pulse the group for how they felt the coaching sessions went. Lead a 5-minute discussion using the debriefing questions below.

Discussion Questions for Debriefing

- How well did you do getting into the discussion?

- Did it help that you were starting with a topic that you knew the performer was interested in (versus something that was on your mind)?

- As the performer, did you notice your coachability go up and down during the discussion? What were the triggers?

- Would you be willing to share with the group one of the questions your coach asked that you feel was particularly effective?

Learning Activity 15: Quick Start to Critical Thinking

LEARNING ACTIVITY 15

Quick Start to Critical Thinking

Objectives

Participants will be able to

- Identify common questions they can ask to help performers expand their perspective

- Practice using these critical thinking questions in a coaching discussion.

Materials

- Presentation Slides 51-52

- Handout 9: Quick Start to Critical Thinking Worksheet

Time

15-20 minutes

Instructions

1. Divide the group into pairs (with one trio if odd number of participants). You can pair people up with folks at their table so they don't have to move.

2. Pass out Handout 9: Quick Start to Critical Thinking Worksheet to the participants and go over the top portion for performers.

3. Ask each person to circle one item in the "performer" portion. This should take just a minute or two.

4. Go over the remaining items on the worksheet and ask pairs to switch sheets. Ask each pair to determine who will be the coach and who will be the performer.

Learning Activity 15, *continued*

LEARNING ACTIVITY 15, continued

5. Direct each coach to interview the performer using these questions on the worksheet. The coach should take notes on the worksheet for the performer. Each round of interviews is 5 minutes, so let participants know when 3 minutes and then 5 minutes have passed.

6. Then ask partners to switch roles and repeat process in step 5. Once the two rounds of interviews are complete, ask pairs to return handouts so that each performer has his or her sheet back with notes from the conversation.

7. Take about 5 minutes to process the activity. Use the questions on the slide and below to help guide your discussion.

Discussion Questions for Debriefing

- Did you find that these questions helped you expand your thinking about your problem or challenge? Why or why not?

- Which question was most helpful to you? (Take a poll, asking participants to raise hands so they see that each person might need a different question.)

- If a peer asked you these same questions tomorrow, would you remain coachable? (Some people might find these questions challenging and get defensive, so question is good to explore.)

- If you would like your team members to do more peer-level coaching, might you want to use this exercise at your next staff meeting? What's the downside? (The upside is that by making it an exercise, you might reduce the angst of the inquiry and increase coachability.)

Chapter 13
Assessments

What's in This Chapter

- Assessments to use in your workshops in thumbnail format for reference
- Facilitator assessment for professional development
- Refer to Chapter 15 for instructions to download full-size assessments

Using assessments during a workshop has the potential to help participants identify areas of strength and weakness so that they can capitalize on their strengths, improve their weaknesses, and ultimately perform better in the workplace. The coaching workshops featured in this book are practice driven and as such have been designed to include two assessment tools for the participants. The first assessment, the Coaching Skills Diagnostic, is used during the one-day and two-day workshops to help participants build self-awareness about their coaching skills. The second, shorter assessment on uncoachability provides a checklist for participants to build self-awareness of the triggers that might diminish their ability to *receive* coaching.

Assessments can also help you identify your areas of strength and weakness as a facilitator. Assessment 3 provides an instrument to help you manage your professional development and increase the effectiveness of your training sessions. You can use this instrument in a number of ways: self-assessment, end-of-course feedback, observer feedback, or as a gauge for tracking professional growth with repeated ratings.

The instruments in this chapter provide instructions on how to complete the assessments and when to use them in the course of the workshop. See Chapter 15 for complete instructions on how to download full-size versions of these workshop assessments.

Assessments Included in *Coaching Training*

Assessment 1. Coaching Skills Diagnostic

Assessment 2. Uncoachability Triggers Checklist

Assessment 3: Facilitator Competencies

Assessment 1: Coaching Skills Diagnostic

Coaching Skills Diagnostic

Instructions: Read through each item and place an "X" in first or second column based on your self-assessment. After you have done this for all items, review your responses and place an "X" in the last column for the two or three items on which you would most like to focus.

Item	Hmm... I Need to Work on This	Strength: I got this!	My Focus Few
I am able to focus on what someone is saying and take it in with interest (I don't get easily distracted or start practicing my response before person stops talking).			
When I am coaching someone, I make sure he or she does most of the talking.			
I do not interrupt others when they talk, even if I feel I understand what they are trying to say.			
I am honestly very interested in what other people are up to (their goals). I think everyone is fascinating in some way.			
I am able to help uncoachable people open up and become coachable (for example, when someone seems defensive or uninterested).			
When I coach people, I let them own the discussion and determine how I can best help (versus me leading).			
Once I have determined that I want to offer to coach someone, I feel pretty comfortable approaching the person and starting the discussion.			
I ask great questions that engage others and help inspire bigger thinking.			
When I coach someone, he or she generally leaves the conversation feeling better than when it began.			

Assessment 1, *continued*

Item	Hmm... I Need to Work on This	Strength: I got this!	My Focus Few
When I coach others, I help them discover and define where they want to go to attain their goals (vision, the path forward).			
I know how to coach someone who is feeling stuck or overwhelmed.			
I am a "yes, go for it" person, not the type that says "yes, but," so much that the person gets frustrated (for example, always plays devil's advocate).			
I feel comfortable helping others broaden their perspective when they are unable to see what's slowing their progress.			
I help those I coach create an action plan that they own and feel highly motivated to implement.			
I feel comfortable managing agreements to hold others accountable for their intentions and promises without it seeming like I have taken over ownership.			
I excel at helping others discover their strengths and apply them.			
I am able to "shape-shift" to meet the needs of those I coach (show up in a variety of ways depending on what they most need).			
People seek out my coaching (this is different from seeking my advice).			

Overall impression of your self-assessment:

Assessment 2: Uncoachability Triggers Checklist

Uncoachability Triggers Checklist

Instructions: The following are common triggers that reduce coachability for some people, some of the time. Check any item that has impacted your coachability in the last month. If you can't recall a specific situation, check off the triggers you know can affect whether you seek or hear coaching or input. Note that it is normal to check off several triggers—we're human afterall! The purpose of this exercise is to help you recognize common triggers so that you can catch yourself as you are becoming less coachable and choose a more open stance.

I have become less coachable when someone offered coaching......

_____ Too early in the morning/day
_____ Too late in the afternoon/shift
_____ When I am on break
_____ On Monday/first shift of the week
_____ On Friday/last shift of the week
_____ In a group setting
_____ In the hallway when I am on my way somewhere
_____ While they are obviously distracted or multitasking
_____ When I am cold/hot
_____ In my office
_____ In his/her office

I have become less coachable when I feel....

_____ Tired
_____ Overwhelmed
_____ Like I have to defend myself
_____ It's personal
_____ Stressed
_____ Confused
_____ Unprepared

I am sometimes less coachable when the person....

_____ Is higher on the organization chart than I am
_____ Is lower on the organization chart than I am
_____ Is a peer
_____ Comes across very direct/strong
_____ Talks in generalities
_____ Shares too many details
_____ Comes across too formally
_____ Is long winded
_____ Tells me what I am doing wrong
_____ Is not listening to me

I have become less coachable when....

_____ The topic is not of interest to me
_____ When I don't think improvement is needed
_____ The topic has been discussed many times before

Other Triggers:

Total number of triggers checked off:

Assessment 3: Facilitator Competencies

Facilitator Competencies

This assessment instrument will help you as the facilitator manage your professional development and increase the effectiveness of your coaching training sessions. You can use this instrument in the following ways:

Self-assessment. Use the assessment to rate yourself on the five-point scale, which will generate an overall profile and help determine the competency areas that are in the greatest need of improvement.

End-of-course feedback. Honest feedback from the training participants can lessen the possibility that facilitators deceive themselves about the 12 competencies. Trainees may not be able to rate the facilitator on all 12, so it may be necessary to ask the participants to rate only those they consider themselves qualified to address.

Observer feedback. Facilitators may observe each other's training sessions and provide highly useful information on the 12 competencies that are crucial to be effective in conducting training.

Repeat ratings. This assessment can be the basis for tracking professional growth on the competencies needed to be an effective facilitator. The repeat measure may be obtained as often as needed to gauge progress on action plans for improvement.

The Competencies

Facilitators are faced with challenges anytime they lead a training session. Many skills are necessary to help participants meet their learning needs and to ensure that the organization achieves its desired results for the training. This assessment contains a set of 12 important competencies that effective coaching training requires. Not all seasoned facilitators have expertise in all of these competencies, but they may represent learning and growth areas for almost any facilitator.

Here is a detailed explanation of the importance of each of the dozen crucial elements of facilitator competence:

Assessment 3, *continued*

Understanding adult learners: Uses knowledge of the principles of adult learning in both designing and delivering training.

Effective facilitators are able to draw on the experiences of the learners in a training session and then give them the applicable content and tools to engage them fully and help them see the value of the learning. It is also important to address the participants' various learning styles and provide them with opportunities to solve problems and think critically so they can work through real business issues and develop additional skills.

Presentation skills: Presents content clearly to achieve the desired outcomes of the training. Encourages learners to generate their own answers through effectively leading group discussions.

Of all the competencies a facilitator uses during a training session, none may be more obvious than the need to have exceptional presentation skills. The facilitator's ability to present content effectively and in an entertaining way is one of the first things learners notice and is a large part of a successful workshop. The nature of adult learning makes it equally important that the facilitator is not just a talking head but is also adept at initiating, drawing out, guiding, and summarizing information gleaned from large-group discussions during a training session. The facilitator's role is not to feed answers to learners as if they are empty vessels waiting to be filled. Rather, it is the facilitator's primary task to generate learning on the part of the participants through their own process of discovery.

Communication skills: Expresses self well, both verbally and in writing. Understands nonverbal communication and listens effectively.

Beyond presenting information and leading discussions, it is vital for a facilitator to be highly skilled in all aspects of communication. He or she should use language that learners can understand; give clear directions for activities; involve trainees through appropriate humor, anecdotes, and examples; and build on the ideas of others. This will lead to training sessions that are engaging and highly valuable for the participants. Facilitators must also be able to listen well and attend to learners' nonverbal communication to create common meaning and mutual understanding.

Assessment 3, *continued*

Emotional intelligence: Respects learners' viewpoints, knowledge, and experience. Recognizes and responds appropriately to others' feelings, attitudes, and concerns.

Because learners may have many different backgrounds, experience levels, and opinions in the same training sessions, facilitators must be able to handle a variety of situations and conversations well, and be sensitive to others' emotions. They must pay close attention to the dynamics in the room, be flexible enough to make immediate changes to activities during training to meet the needs of learners, and create an open and trusting learning environment. Attendees should feel comfortable expressing their opinions, asking questions, and participating in activities without fear of repercussion or disapproval. Monitoring learners' emotions during a training session also helps the facilitator gauge when it may be time to change gears if conflict arises, if discussion needs to be refocused on desired outcomes, or if there is a need to delve deeper into a topic to encourage further learning.

Training methods: Varies instructional approaches to address different learning styles and hold learners' interest.

All trainees have preferred learning styles, and one of the keys to effective training facilitation is to use a variety of methods to address them. Some people are more visual ("see it") learners, and others are more auditory ("hear it") or kinesthetic ("do it") learners. An effective facilitator must be familiar with a variety of training methods to tap into each participant's style(s) and maintain interest during the training session. These methods may include such activities as small-group activities, individual exercises, case studies, role plays, simulations, and games.

Subject matter expertise: Possesses deep knowledge of training content and applicable experience to draw upon.

Facilitators must have solid background knowledge of the training topic at hand and be able to share related experience to help learners connect theory to real-world scenarios. Anecdotes and other examples to illustrate how the training content relates to participants' circumstances and work can enhance the learning experience and encourage learners to apply the information and also to use the tools they have been given. It is also crucial that facilitators know their topics inside and out, so they can answer the trainees' questions and guide them toward problem-solving and skill development.

Assessment 3, *continued*

Questioning skills: Asks questions in a way that stimulates learners' understanding and curiosity. Encourages critical thinking.

An effective questioning technique works well to assess learners' understanding of training content. It also provides opportunities for them to analyze information and think critically. When learners ask questions, the facilitator is able to see where there may be confusion or a need to review concepts for better understanding. Similarly, when a facilitator asks thought-provoking questions in a way that invites participation, learners can brainstorm solutions to problems or think about situations to help them apply the training content to the issues they deal with on a regular basis.

Eliciting behavior change: Influences others effectively both individually and within groups. Gains support and commitment from others to achieve common goals and desired outcomes.

This competency is important in two ways. First, facilitators must be able to persuade trainees to consider points of view that will lead to desired changes in behavior. A facilitator is often called upon to sell an organization's culture or policies, or to gain learners' participation to achieve the desired results of the training. To do this, a facilitator must be able to show that although he or she respects the trainees' views, the trainees must understand and accept the organization's realities and practices.

Second, an effective facilitator must know how to form small groups and work well with them to influence groups to accomplish tasks, work through problems, and fulfill the needs of the group members. Drawing out the creative energy of groups through brainstorming or other activities, as well as helping group members blend their unique knowledge and skills to achieve a common goal, will lead to greater commitment on behalf of the learners to improve their behavior and apply the training content.

Feedback: Gives and receives constructive, specific, and timely feedback, and communicates observations clearly and accurately.

It is essential for facilitators to provide learners with helpful feedback, whether formally through an assessment or informally through conversation. Use specific examples to communicate a learner's strengths and weaknesses; this will help the trainee understand the information and may also increase the learner's self-reflection. It can also serve as the basis for a coaching relationship for individual training and clarify what the learner should focus on for his or her growth and

---

Assessment 3, *continued*

development. The facilitator should also be familiar with a variety of tools to gather feedback from training participants to improve the learning experience and the facilitator's own self-reflection and growth.

Motivation: Encourages learners to participate and achieve desired results. Generates enthusiasm and commitment from others.

It is the training facilitator's responsibility to inspire others to achieve the desired outcomes of a training session and to focus on their goals. Although it is generally believed that motivation comes from within, a skilled facilitator can unleash energy and enthusiasm by creating a vision that inspires the learners. Facilitators can provide meaningful learning activities and infuse fun into the training experience, and they must effectively channel trainees' motivation into a commitment to achieving results.

Organizational skills: Works in an orderly and logical way to accomplish tasks. Ensures that work is correct and complete. Presents ideas logically and sequentially.

The importance of this competency for facilitators is twofold. First, the facilitator must have good work habits and pay attention to detail. With any training event, many factors are necessary to ensure a successful experience. Work must be done thoroughly and accurately. A well-organized training facilitator typically creates well-organized, professional training. Second, it is important for facilitators to present ideas in a logical, sequential order that allows learners to absorb new content easily and also to be able to retrieve it quickly. This also increases the probability that the learners will actually use the content. The more organized the facilitator, the better.

Time management: Plans and uses time effectively. Balances important and urgent tasks and can work on multiple tasks simultaneously.

Facilitators do many things in addition to conducting training sessions. They must also budget their time effectively to address other priorities in their work: prepare for the training, keep accurate records, analyze assessment data, design new content or activities, and report to the client organization. The most competent facilitators are able to multitask and keep the goals of the learners and client organization in view as much as possible. Good time management helps a facilitator keep track of all there is to do during any given day.

Assessment 3, *continued*

Assessment 3, *continued*

ASSESSMENT 3, continued

Facilitator Competencies Assessment

Instructions: If using this instrument as a self-assessment, place a ✓ in the box to the right of each of the 12 facilitator competencies that best describes your skill level. If using this form to provide feedback to a facilitator, place a ✓ in the box that best fits his or her level of competence in each area.

COMPETENCY	EXPECTATIONS				
	None	Little	Some	Adequate	Expert
Understanding adult learners: Uses knowledge of the principles of adult learning when both designing and delivering training.	☐	☐	☐	☐	☐
Presentation skills: Presents content clearly to achieve the desired outcomes of the training. Encourages learners to generate their own answers through effectively leading group discussions.	☐	☐	☐	☐	☐
Communication skills: Expresses self well verbally and in writing. Understands nonverbal communication and listens effectively.	☐	☐	☐	☐	☐
Emotional intelligence: Respects learners' viewpoints, knowledge, and experience. Recognizes and responds appropriately to others' feelings, attitudes, and concerns.	☐	☐	☐	☐	☐
Training methods: Varies instructional approaches to address different learning styles and hold learners' interest.	☐	☐	☐	☐	☐
Subject matter expertise: Possesses deep knowledge of training content and applicable experience to draw upon.	☐	☐	☐	☐	☐

Original material by Lisa Haneberg, © 2015 Association for Talent Development (ATD). Used with permission.

COACHING training 6

COMPETENCY	EXPECTATIONS				
	None	Little	Some	Adequate	Expert
Questioning skills: Asks questions in a way that stimulates learners' understanding and curiosity. Encourages critical thinking.	☐	☐	☐	☐	☐
Eliciting behavior change: Influences others effectively, both individually and within groups. Gains support and commitment from others to achieve common goals and desired outcomes.	☐	☐	☐	☐	☐
Feedback: Gives and receives constructive, specific, and timely feedback and communicates observations clearly and accurately.	☐	☐	☐	☐	☐
Motivation: Encourages learners to participate and achieve desired results. Generates enthusiasm and commitment from others.	☐	☐	☐	☐	☐
Organizational skills: Works in an orderly and logical way to accomplish tasks. Ensures work is correct and complete. Presents ideas logically and sequentially for learners to understand.	☐	☐	☐	☐	☐
Time management: Plans time effectively. Balances important and urgent tasks and can work on multiple tasks simultaneously.	☐	☐	☐	☐	☐

Original material by Lisa Haneberg, © 2015 Association for Talent Development (ATD). Used with permission.

COACHING training 7

Chapter 14
Handouts

What's in This Chapter

- Ten handouts to use in your workshops
- Refer to Chapter 15 for instructions to download full-sized handouts

Handouts comprise the various materials you will provide to the learners throughout the course of the workshop. In some cases, the handouts will simply provide instructions for worksheets to complete, places to take notes, and so forth. In other cases, they will provide important and practical materials for use in and out of the training room, such as reference materials, tip sheets, samples of completed forms, flowcharts, and so forth.

The workshop agendas in Chapters 1–3 and the learning activities in Chapter 12 will provide instructions for how and when to use the handouts within the context of the workshop. See Chapter 15 for complete instructions on how to download the workshop support materials.

Handouts Included in *Coaching Training*

Handout 1. Coaching Model

Handout 2. Coaching Roles

Handout 3. Conversation Characteristics That Create Pull

Handout 4. My Coaching Worksheet

Handout 5. Practice 1 Coaching Worksheet

Handout 6. Critical Thinking Worksheet

Handout 7. Practice 2 Coaching Worksheet

Handout 8. Getting Started Practice Worksheet

Handout 9. Quick Start to Critical Thinking Worksheet

Handout 10. Workshop Evaluation Form

Handout 1. Coaching Model

HANDOUT 1

Coaching Model

Performer's Role

| Conversation | Perspective |
| Coachability | Progress |

Coach's Role

COACHING training   1

Handout 1, *continued*

HANDOUT 1, continued

Conversation

Coaching occurs in conversation, so conversation is the core tool you have for providing great coaching. To enhance conversations:

- **Listen deeply.** Show interest, don't be distracted, and focus on the performer.
- **Ask great questions.**
- **Create** *pull.*
  - Use a rallying cry that "rallies"
  - Be evocative—encourage reflection and bring out pride
  - Be provocative—excite, fascinate, and intrigue
  - Be memorable in some way
  - Make people feel great—bring out their awesomeness
  - Improve relationships and connection
  - Help people see the way forward—be catalytic
  - Provide advocacy—pave the way with some assistance

Perspective

One of the most valuable coaching services you can provide is to help performers adopt a healthy perspective about their situation. This is most needed when performers feel overwhelmed, unsuccessful, stuck, hassled, unconfident, or unworthy. Ask about the performer's:

- Amount of information
- Multiple points of view
- Worries
- Interconnectedness
- Capacity and skills
- Potential alternative paths.

Coachability

Coachability is measured by how performers interact with their environment. It is visible, observable behavior. Coachability:

- Is not defensive when challenged
- Welcomes feedback and ideas for improvement
- Asks for coaching
- Considers and uses ideas offered by others
- Seeks training and development in the form of reading, classes, new assignments, and coaching from others
- Has a good sense of own strengths and weaknesses
- Handles failures and setbacks with grace.

Progress

Many performers do not lack vision, but some fail to produce satisfactory results due to inadequate progress. Progress, even in small amounts, is one of the most powerful motivators we can tap into. Coaches enable progress by helping performers create a plan, managing agreements, and inspiring action. Ask:

- What's the next step? What's the first action for this step?
- What requests could you make to move things forward?
- What conversations could you have, and with whom, to get things moving?
- What can I do to help jumpstart your progress?

COACHING training   2

Handout 2. Coaching Roles

HANDOUT 2

Coaching Roles

Performer's Role

| Conversation | Perspective |
| Coachability | Progress |

Coach's Role

→ Great coaching starts here!

Performer's Role: The performer is the one who should own and seek coaching. And when coaching is offered, performers should be open to and pull in coaching. The performer's goals or interests are the focus for coaching. The key to receiving great coaching is being coachable.

- Be coachable.
- Have a goal you want to work on.
- Seek coaching. Ask for the type of help you feel you need. Be open to the idea that you might need something else entirely.
- Let others influence you. Use the input and ideas you receive—consider it all, even if you don't do it all.
- Own your progress. It is not the coach's job to motivate you or hold you accountable.

Coach's Role: The coach is the one who helps. Period. Coaching is a service-oriented act with the goal of helping the performer make progress on one of his or her goals or interests. The key to delivering great coaching is to be whoever is needed to be most helpful, which can be both exhilarating and daunting.

- Listen deeply; show interest.
- Provide great service.
- Offer coaching; say yes to coaching.
- Help the performer clarify goals, get unstuck, make a connection, see something in a new way, uncover alternative paths, build self-awareness, and move forward.

COACHING training

Handout 3. Conversation Characteristics That Create Pull

HANDOUT 3

Conversation Characteristics That Create Pull

Use Rallying Cry That Rallies	Emphasize overarching messages that are meaningful to the performer. For example, many senior leaders make the mistake of using profitability as a rallying cry, but many frontline employees are not motivated by this and could even be repelled by it (their hard work is buying the boss's new BMW).
Be Evocative	Use messages that encourage reflection and ask the performer to recall their experiences. Evocation tends to bring out a sense of pride or importance. For example, you might ask, "Why did you first get into this line of work?" Or "What have you done in the past that has worked well for you?"
Be Provocative	Spark attention. As a coach, share examples, stories, and resources that the performer finds exciting, fascinating, or intriguing. For example, share an article or video that highlights cutting-edge ideas related to the performer's goal. Invite the performer to hear an author speak or to a local workshop.
Be Memorable	Ensure coaching has impact beyond the coaching conversation and is memorable. Share a great metaphor, role model courage, be funny, or use a great mantra or key phrase. For example, "Coaches should listen deeply" and "Performers should be coachable" are mantras for this workshop.
Make people feel great	Help performers feel good about themselves because that will help them be more coachable and motivated to do what's needed to progress. Show admiration and appreciation; acknowledge performers' strengths and experiences to help bolster their confidence and resolve. Do this sincerely—we all have our own brand of amazing.
Improve relationships and connection	Coaching occurs in conversation and is relationship based. Strengthen the bond between coach and performer as well as between the performer and others. When we feel connected to someone, we pull into their world and choose to spend time with them.
Help people see the way forward	Give performers hope and vision, which can be catalytic. Performers will seek and pull into conversations that they find helpful and make them feel more confident and clear about what's next. Coaching is, at its core, a conversation that helps performers make progress. To do this, they need to see the future.
Provide advocacy	Recognize and take opportunities to advocate on behalf of the performer—but only if the performer welcomes it. Advocacy means taking initiative to represent the performer's goals, which can be one of the most helpful and powerful things you can do for the performer.

PULL is better than PUSH!

COACHING training

Handout 4. My Coaching Worksheet

HANDOUT 4

My Coaching Worksheet

"Performer" Role
You are about to receive some coaching. Awesome! Take this opportunity to seek and pull into coaching by identifying the topic for the coaching. Complete the following planning questions. Please note that you will be sharing this worksheet with your coach.

A Goal or Interest:
Write down one goal or interest you have and about which you would welcome coaching. Here are a few examples: I want to earn a promotion. I want to spend more time in leisure or recharging my batteries. I want to increase my influence with peers/leaders/others. I want to help my team be more agile. I want to manage stress better.

I want to:

Why is this important to you?

Are you coachable right now? ___Yes ___ No. (If not, what can you say to yourself right now to be more coachable? Say that.)

Original material by Lisa Haneberg. © 2015 Association for Talent Development (ATD). Used with permission.

COACHING training

Handout 5. Practice 1 Coaching Worksheet

HANDOUT 5

Practice 1 Coaching Worksheet

The Performer's Goal:

Starting the Coaching Discussion: How might you start the coaching discussion? Jot down two or three ideas here and then circle the approach you like the most and will use during the practice.

Creating PULL: Refer to your workshop materials and write down three ways you can try to create more *pull* during the practice. While you cannot do many of the things you could do in a live coaching session (such as show a video or take the performer to a talk), you should have no problem brainstorming several ways you can increase *pull* during this exercise.

Great Questions: Write down two great questions to use during the coaching session that will help improve the coaching conversation.

Remember that job number one is to listen deeply. Let the performer do most of the talking.

Original material by Lisa Haneberg. © 2015 Association for Talent Development (ATD). Used with permission.

COACHING training

Handout 6. Critical Thinking Worksheet

HANDOUT 6

Critical Thinking Worksheet

Performer: List a problem or challenge you are struggling with.

Coach: Use these questions to "interview" the performer. Take a few notes about his or her responses (you will return the form to the performer). It is fine if you don't get through all the questions. Go where the energy is.

Information: Do you have the information you need to move forward? Do key stakeholders have the information they need?

Points of View: Have you collected input from various points of view? If you could partner with anyone, who would you engage? How does the "customer" view this problem or challenge?

Worries: What are you most worried about? Are your worries justified?

Interconnectedness: How are other functions or processes connected to this one? How could you strengthen the alignment between these parts?

Capacity: Do you have the capacity needed to be successful? How might you increase capacity? Where are the bottlenecks?

Alternative Paths: What would make it OK to pursue another avenue or approach? Who is most invested in this path? What's their/your interest? Will another path meet the interest?

Original material by Lisa Haneberg. © 2015 Association for Talent Development (ATD). Used with permission.

COACHING training

Handout 7. Practice 2 Coaching Worksheet

HANDOUT 7

Practice 2 Coaching Worksheet

The Performer's Goal:

Increasing Coachability: You might not know the performer you are practicing with, but you can still plan for ways you can increase performer coachability. Refer to your workshop materials on coachability and jot down two or three ideas for things you might be able to do to enhance the performer's openness to your coaching.

Creating PULL: Refer to your workshop materials and write down two or three ways you can try to create more *pull* during the practice. While you cannot do many of the things you could do in a live coaching session (such as show a video or take the performer to a talk), you should have no problem brainstorming several ways you can increase pull during this exercise.

Great Questions: Write down two great questions to use during the coaching session that will help improve the coaching conversation.

Remember that job number one is to listen deeply. Let the performer do most of the talking.

Original material by Lisa Haneberg. © 2015 Association for Talent Development (ATD). Used with permission.

COACHING training 1

Handout 7, continued

HANDOUT 7, continued

The Performer's Goal:

Provide Perspective: Reflect on the performer's goal. What might be some of the ways you can help expand the performer's perspective about this topic? Use the Critical Thinking Worksheet (Handout 6) from the previous exercise for ideas. For example, if the performer wants to reduce stress, you might try exploring what he or she might be worried about and the performer's capacity to achieve his or her goals. If the goal is related to career growth, you might explore the questions listed under information and interconnectedness. Jot down two questions related to perspective that you will use during the practice.

Ensure Performer Progress: Ask one or more of the following questions after the instructor indicates there are just a few minutes left to the practice. Or write down your own question that will help the performer transition into next steps.

- What's the next step? What's the first action for this step?
- What requests could you make to move things forward?
- What conversations could you have, and with whom, to get things moving?
- What can I do to help jumpstart your progress?

Original material by Lisa Haneberg, © 2015 Association for Talent Development (ATD). Used with permission. COACHING training 2

Handout 8. Getting Started Practice Worksheet

HANDOUT 8

Getting Started Practice Worksheet

Performer: Circle one topic that resonates with you most and about which you are interested in receiving coaching.

I want to earn a promotion.

I want to spend more time in leisure or recharging my batteries.

I want to increase my influence with peers/leaders/others.

I want to help my team be more agile.

I want to manage stress better.

I want to be a better listener.

I want to do more coaching.

I want to write a book.

I want to complete a marathon.

I want to spend more time being proactive versus reactive.

I want to be a better presenter.

Starting the Coaching Discussion: How might you start the coaching discussion? Jot down two or three ideas here and then circle the approach you like the most and will use during the practice.

Great Questions: Write down two great questions to use during the coaching session that will help improve the coaching conversation.

Coaches: Remember that job number one is to listen deeply. Let the performer do most of the talking.

Original material by Lisa Haneberg, © 2015 Association for Talent Development (ATD). Used with permission. COACHING training

Handout 9. Quick Start to Critical Thinking Worksheet

HANDOUT 9

Quick Start to Critical Thinking Worksheet

Performer: Circle one topic or challenge that resonates with you most and about which you are interested in receiving coaching.

I am not getting things done on time.

I feel overwhelmed.

I can't seem to persuade decision makers.

I feel stuck in my role; I'm not growing or moving forward.

I am not using my strengths at work.

I am struggling to engage my team.

I feel a bit intimidated by this approach to coaching.

Coach: Use these questions to "interview" the performer. Take a few notes about their responses (you will return the form to the performer). It is fine if you don't get through all the questions. Go where the energy is.

Do you have the information you need to move forward? If not, what do you need?

Do stakeholders have the information they need? If not, what should you communicate?

If you could partner with anyone, who would you engage?

What are you most worried about? Are your worries justified?

What would make it OK to pursue another avenue or approach?

Do you have the capacity needed to be successful? How might you increase capacity?

Where are the bottlenecks?

Original material by Lisa Haneberg, © 2015 Association for Talent Development (ATD). Used with permission. COACHING training

Handout 10. Workshop Evaluation Form

HANDOUT 10

Workshop Evaluation Form

Session Title: _____

Trainer: _____ **Date:** _____

Instructions: Circle the number that best corresponds to how you feel about the workshop. Please write additional comments below the table. Your insights make a difference!

Question	1 Not Useful	2 Somewhat Useful	3 Very Useful
How useful was the session in helping you build your skills and confidence to coach others?	1	2	3
How useful were the group exercises?	1	2	3
How knowledgeable was the facilitator?	1	2	3
How effective was the facilitator?	1	2	3

What did you like best about the workshop?

What would you like to recommend concerning this workshop for future participants?

What will you do differently as a result of this session?

Do you have other comments regarding the training experience? Share below!

Original material by Lisa Haneberg, © 2015 Association for Talent Development (ATD). Used with permission. COACHING training

Chapter 15

Online Tools and Downloads

What's in This Chapter

- Instructions to access supporting materials
- Options for using tools and downloads
- Licensing and copyright information for workshop programs
- Tips for working with the downloaded files

The ATD Workshop Series is designed to give you flexible options for many levels of training facilitation and topic expertise. As you prepare your program, you will want to incorporate many of the handouts, assessments, presentation slides, and other training tools provided as supplementary materials with this volume. We wish you the best of luck in delivering your training workshops. It is exciting work that ultimately can change lives.

Access to Free Supporting Materials

To get started, visit the ATD Workshop Series page: www.td.org/workshopbooks. This page includes links to download all the free supporting materials that accompany this book, as well as up-to-date information about additions to the series and new program offerings.

These downloads, which are included in the price of the book, feature ready-to-use learning activities, handouts, assessments, and presentation slide files in PDF format. Use these files to deliver your workshop program and as a resource to help you prepare your own materials. You may download and use any of these files as part of your training delivery for the workshops, provided no changes are made to the original materials. To access this material, you will be asked to log into the ATD website. If you are not an ATD member, you will have to create an ATD account.

If you choose to re-create these documents, they can only be used within your organization; they cannot be presented or sold as your original work. Please note that all materials included in the book are copyrighted and you are using them with permission of ATD. If you choose to re-create the materials, per copyright usage requirements, you must provide attribution to the original source of the content and display a copyright notice as follows:

Customizable Materials

You can also choose to customize this supporting content for an additional licensing fee. This option gives you access to a downloadable zip file with the entire collection of supporting materials in Microsoft Word and PowerPoint file formats. Once purchased, you will have indefinite and unlimited access to these materials through the My Downloads section of your ATD account. Then, you will be able to customize and personalize all the documents and presentations using Microsoft Word and PowerPoint. You can add your own content, change the order or format, include your company logo, or make any other customization.

Please note that all the original documents contain attribution to ATD and this book as the original source for the material. As you customize the documents, remember to keep these attributions intact (see the copyright notice above). By doing so, you are practicing professional courtesy by respecting the intellectual property rights of another trainer (the author) and modeling respect for copyright and intellectual property laws for your program participants.

ATD offers two custom material license options: Internal Use and Client Use. To determine which license option you need to purchase, ask yourself the following question:

Will I or my employer be charging a person or outside organization a fee for providing services or for delivering training that includes any ATD Workshop content that you wish to customize?

If the answer is yes, then you need to purchase a Client Use license.

If the answer is no, and you plan to customize ATD Workshop content to deliver training at no cost to employees within your own department or company only, you need to purchase the Internal Use license.

Working with the Files

PDF Documents

To read or print the PDF files you download, you must have PDF reader software such as Adobe Acrobat Reader installed on your system. The program can be downloaded free of cost from the Adobe website: www.adobe.com. To print documents, simply use the PDF reader to open the downloaded files and print as many copies as you need.

PowerPoint Slides

To use or adapt the contents of the PowerPoint presentation files (available with the Internal Use and Client Use licenses), you must have Microsoft PowerPoint software installed on your system. If you simply want to view the PowerPoint documents, you only need an appropriate viewer on your system. Microsoft provides various viewers for free download at www.microsoft.com.

Once you have downloaded the files to your computer system, use Microsoft PowerPoint (or free viewer) to print as many copies of the presentation slides as you need. You can also make handouts of the presentations by choosing the "print three slides per page" option on the print menu.

You can modify or otherwise customize the slides by opening and editing them in Microsoft PowerPoint. However, you must retain the credit line denoting the original source of the material, as noted earlier in this chapter. It is illegal to present this content as your own work. The files will open as read-only files, so before you adapt them you will need to save them onto your hard drive.

The PowerPoint slides included in this volume support the three workshop agendas:

- Two-Day Workshop
- One-Day Workshop
- Half-Day Workshop

For PowerPoint slides to successfully support and augment your learning program, it is essential that you practice giving presentations with the slides *before* using them in live training situations. You should be confident that you can logically expand on the points featured in the presentations and discuss the methods for working through them. If you want to fully engage your participants, become familiar with this technology before you use it. See the text box that follows for a cheat sheet to help you navigate through the presentation. A good practice is to insert comments into PowerPoint's notes feature, which you can print out and use when you present the slides. The workshop agendas in this book show thumbnails of each slide to help you keep your place as you deliver the workshop.

NAVIGATING THROUGH A POWERPOINT PRESENTATION	
Key	**PowerPoint "Show" Action**
Space bar or Enter or Mouse click	Advance through custom animations embedded in the presentation
Backspace	Back up to the last projected element of the presentation
Escape	Abort the presentation
B or b	Blank the screen to black
B or b (repeat)	Resume the presentation
W or w	Blank the screen to white
W or w (repeat)	Resume the presentation

About the Author

Lisa Haneberg is an organization development, leadership, and management author, trainer, researcher, practitioner, and consultant. She has more than 25 years of experience providing executive and management development training and coaching solutions for large and small organizations (including health care, manufacturing, services, nonprofit, and government organizations). She has particular expertise in the areas of senior team development, performance management, coaching, talent management, succession planning, organizational agility and alignment, and middle management effectiveness.

Lisa has written extensively on these topics. Among her many books are *Organization Development Basics* (ASTD Press), *Coaching Basics* (ASTD Press), *10 Steps to Be a Successful Manager* (ASTD Press), *Developing Great Managers: 20 Power Hours* (ASTD Press), *The High Impact Middle Manager: Powerful Strategies to Thrive in the Middle* (ASTD Press), *High Impact Middle Management: Solutions for Today's Busy Public-Sector Managers* (ASTD Press), *Coaching Up and Down the Generations* (ASTD Press and Berrett-Koehler), and *The Management Development Handbook* (ASTD Press).

In addition, Lisa's work has been highlighted in publications such as *Leader to Leader, Washington CEO, Capital,* and *Leadership Excellence.* She is a nationally recognized thought leader and speaker. In 2011, she won the HCI M-Prize for management innovation (a competition judged by management legend Gary Hamel).

Lisa has held both internal and external consulting roles in organizations such as Memorial Hermann Health System, MedCentral, Black & Decker, Mead Paper, Intel, Amazon.com, Corbis, Promedica, MTD Products, Perfetti vanMelle, TUI Travel International, Aultman Health Care, OPW Fueling Components, Royal Thai Government, the FAA, the EPA, Microsoft, Premera Blue Cross Oregon, and the City of Seattle. She holds a bachelor's degree in behavioral sciences from the University of Maryland and a master's degree in fine arts from Goddard College.

To learn more about Lisa's work, visit www.lisahaneberg.com and read her popular blog: Management Craft www.managementcraft.com.

About ATD

The Association for Talent Development (ATD), formerly ASTD, is the world's largest association dedicated to those who develop talent in organizations. These professionals help others achieve their full potential by improving their knowledge, skills, and abilities.

ATD's members come from more than 120 countries and work in public and private organizations in every industry sector.

ATD supports the work of professionals locally in more than 125 chapters, international strategic partners, and global member networks.

atd Association for
Talent Development

1640 King Street
Alexandria, VA 22314
www.td.org
800.628.2783
703.683.8100

HOW TO PURCHASE ATD PRESS PUBLICATIONS

ATD Press publications are available worldwide in print and electronic format.

To place an order, please visit our online store: www.td.org/books.

Our publications are also available at select online and brick-and-mortar retailers.

Outside the United States, English-language ATD Press titles may be purchased through the following distributors:

United Kingdom, Continental Europe, the Middle East, North Africa, Central Asia, and Latin America
Eurospan Group
Phone: 44.1767.604.972
Fax: 44.1767.601.640
Email: eurospan@turpin-distribution.com
Website: www.eurospanbookstore.com

Asia
Cengage Learning Asia Pte. Ltd.
Email: asia.info@cengage.com
Website: www.cengageasia.com

Nigeria
Paradise Bookshops
Phone: 08033075133
Email: paradisebookshops@gmail.com
Website: www.paradisebookshops.com

South Africa
Knowledge Resources
Ground Floor, Yellowwood House,
Ballywoods Office Park
33 Ballyclare Drive, Bryanston, South Africa
Phone: +27 (11) 706.6009
Fax: +27 (11) 706.1127
Email: sharon@knowres.co.za
Web: www.kr.co.za

For all other territories, customers may place their orders at the ATD online store: **www.td.org/books**

02157062220